The Graduate Journey

Lessons, Growth & Grace

Odinaka Chukwu Anumudu

The Graduate Journey

Lessons, Growth & Grace

Biblical references and quotations include the use of the following versions: NLT (New Living Translation), AMP (Amplified Version), ISV (International Standard Version), RSV (Revised Standard Version), and NIV (New International Version).

ISBN: 979-8-9871742-7-2
Published in 2025 by The Writer's Writer Studio
Thewriterswriter.org
hello@thewriterswriter.org

In partnership with:
Onefirm Media Corp.
PO Box 186
New York, NY 10031

Contents

Dedication

To my husband, Henry—for walking this journey with me, every step of the way.

Foreword

Some journeys are measured not just in miles crossed or degrees earned, but in the people who walk alongside us, even from one step ahead. My own graduate school path at the University of Pennsylvania's Graduate School of Education began a year after Odinaka's. Yet, her presence—steady, generous, and full of light—made it feel as though I was never truly alone, even when the world went remote.

When I left Nigeria in 2021, leaving behind my husband and two young daughters in the middle of a pandemic, I knew I was stepping into something transformative. But I also feared the loneliness that possibly lay ahead. Graduate school abroad promises opportunity and growth, but it also asks much of us: the courage to uproot, the humility to in some sense start over, and the resilience to keep showing up when the weight of distance and difference grows heavy. For me, there were many days when the silence of separation pressed in, when deadlines loomed larger than life, and when even simple questions felt overwhelming.

Our stories have many parallels, though each is uniquely

ours. Like Ody, I completed my undergraduate studies in Nigeria, earning the same first degree in Economics, before being drawn by a compelling passion into the field of education. Ultimately, I found myself in the same International Educational Development program at the University of Pennsylvania. We both made the difficult choice to leave significant others behind in Nigeria to pursue graduate studies in the US, carrying with us the longing for the communities we had built at home. And, of course, both of us discovered, sometimes with shock, how our physical lifestyles had to change with the move, a truth Ody captures so honestly in her reflections. These parallels reminded me again and again that while every journey is personal, shared experiences can create a quiet, sustaining camaraderie that stretches across borders.

Amid all the deadlines, time differences, and moments of uncertainty, one of the most profound lessons I learned, and that I see reflected in Ody's story, was to fully trust in God for all our tomorrows. Graduate school abroad, especially as an international student leaving family behind, is filled with sudden twists and moments of seemingly endless uncertainty. Yet, it is precisely in these moments when plans shift, visas hang in the balance, or life simply feels unpredictable that faith becomes a steady anchor. Ody's journey reminds us that while we can prepare, plan, and persevere, it is trust in God, as well as an unshakable certainty of his desire for us to have good, that carries us through the unknown.

For me, Ody was not just a storyteller of this experience but a living embodiment of it. In many of those moments, Ody's counsel became a beacon of hope and very often, a compass. Though we were not in the same cohort, she offered guidance as someone who had walked the path just ahead of me. She shared insights about navigating professors' expectations, walked me through assignments that initially seemed impossible, and created space for conversations that reminded me I was more than just a student; I was still a mother, a wife, and a woman carrying both ambition and longing. Her support was practical, yes, but also profoundly human. She reminded me that, as she herself writes, *"We all need humans."*

Ody's journey became a reminder of sorts. She was the friend who showed what it looked like to navigate the program with grace, humor, and resilience, offering guidance and encouragement that made the unfamiliar feel possible. Because of her example, I found myself doing the same for someone who came into the program after me: sharing insights, offering support, and creating space for questions and reflections. In this way, Ody's influence extended far beyond her own experience, reminding me that the generosity of one person can ripple outward, helping others find their footing in a challenging, transformative journey.

This book captures that truth beautifully. *The Graduate Journey* is more than a memoir; it is a mirror for every international student who has wrestled with the uncertainty of applications, the nail-biting wait for decisions, the fervent prayers over visas, and the delicate dance of beginning again in *"another man's land."* Ody does not shy away from the hard parts: culture shock, financial strain, time differences that ache in the bones; yet, she also highlights the unexpected joys: friendships that transcend borders, faith that deepens under pressure, and resilience built step by step.

One of the gifts of this book is its dual nature. It is at once deeply personal and profoundly practical. The chapters invite you into Ody's lived experience, while the Graduate

Journey Toolkit provides concrete resources for anyone considering a similar path. That balance between narrative and guidance is rare. Readers will find both comfort in her honesty and empowerment in her practical advice.

I am honored to write this foreword because Ody's journey is not hers alone. It is the story of countless international students who set out on the uncertain road of graduate education. It is a story of resilience, of faith, of building community across borders, and of finding strength in unexpected places, especially in another's kindness.

For those of us who have walked this road, these pages feel like a companion whispering, *"You made it. You are not alone."* For those preparing to begin, they are a roadmap marked with lessons learned, wisdom shared, and encouragement freely given.

—Adeiye Oluwaseun-Sobo, M.S.Ed
Education Practitioner | UPenn '21 Alum

Introduction

It's been over five years since I packed my bags and moved to the US to begin my graduate studies. Yet, the memories of 2019 still feel like yesterday.

This is one journey that has marked my life in ways that words may never fully capture. I only hope I have done my best, through this book, to put into words the moments that shaped me.

We often think that the graduate school journey begins from the moment one starts the application process. In reality, it starts much earlier—from the years of effort, preparation, and layered experiences that shape your story and eventually flow into your personal statement.

In 2019, I received the prestigious Penn-UNESCO scholarship to study International Educational Development at the University of Pennsylvania (UPenn), becoming the first Nigerian and one of only two recipients that year. UPenn—an Ivy League institution ranked alongside Harvard as the top Graduate School of Education in the United

States—felt like a dream come true. It was truly a surreal moment for me!

I also received a Penn Graduate School of Education Merit Scholarship and became a two-time P.E.O. International Peace Scholar for women committed to education and development. These awards were life-changing, but they also brought a new set of challenges I hadn't fully anticipated.

From the moment I entered graduate school, life became a rollercoaster of activities. However, when the world shut down in 2020 due to COVID-19, I found myself with the space to pause and reflect on my life and journey so far.

I'll never forget the date: it was March 2020. I was in Pittsburgh visiting a member of the P.E.O. Scholarship chapter. I remember thinking how rejuvenating it was and how I should have more outings like it. Little did I know that in the next 24 hours, my life would change dramatically.

The next day, I woke up to a text from my campus residence: everyone was to vacate within the next couple of days. The nation had just announced an official lockdown. I immediately cut short my visit and took the next available bus back to campus.

Upon returning, I couldn't believe it was the same place I had left just a few days earlier. So much had changed in such a short time. The once vibrant halls were now filled with uncertainty and dread as students packed their bags. No one knew when or if we'd return. There were whispers of borders closing, empty grocery shelves, and rising infection rates. It felt like the world as we knew it was coming to a halt.

International students like me, who couldn't leave right away, were granted a few additional days to make travel arrangements. It was scary. But we all tried to be hopeful, convincing ourselves that the situation was temporary and that soon we would be back together, like nothing ever changed.

Academic expectations had to be reassessed in light of the new circumstances: classes shifted online, and I was now confined to my room, 24/7, till it was safe to go out again.

In that precarious situation, I started to think about life and my graduate journey so far. Never had I imagined experiencing such sudden changes in such a short period. All the emotions of the first few months of graduate school started to wash over me, and so, to process my experiences, I picked up my phone and started recording my thoughts. Those voice notes eventually became the Graduate Journey Podcast[1], a space where I shared my vulnerable stories as an international student to remind others that they weren't alone on their respective journeys.

What began as a way to process my own experiences soon became a source of encouragement and validation for others. Listeners, friends, and strangers alike reached out, sharing similar stories and struggles. I realized that, despite our different circumstances, we were all connected in our shared hopes, challenges, and successes.

With each person who shared their story with me, it dawned on me I was never alone in the things I'd gone through. This kind of safe space was something I had longed for at the start of my journey; I had often wished for a community to lean on.

After graduating in 2021, I saw even more people share on public platforms (i.e., YouTube) about the joys and chal-

---

1. The Graduate Journey Podcast is available on podcast platforms. You will find links in the Resources section of this book.

of being an international student. I finally understood that sharing these experiences helped people feel seen while empowering them with the courage to overcome their fears about graduate school. Inspired by this, I decided to not only record my stories on a podcast but to write a book about my graduate journey.

This book began as a way to share my story, but while writing, I decided I also wanted it to be a practical resource for anyone navigating the graduate school journey, especially as an international student. Whether you're just considering graduate school or you are already deep in the process, my goal is to walk you through it all.

I hope that as you read, you see bits and pieces of yourself in the pages of my story. I hope that this book validates your journey and reminds you that you are never alone. I pray it strengthens your faith in God and encourages you for the road ahead. May it build resilience in you, not just for the graduate school journey, but for every situation that pops up in the process of becoming an international student.

Above all, I hope you realize how much you are loved by God. He sees you and is present with you—every step of the way.

Part One

Chapter 1

The Beginning

You saw me before I was born. Every day of my life was recorded in your book. Every moment was laid out before a single day had passed (Psalm 139:16, NLT).

I struggled to make sense of the first two years of my undergraduate studies. I remember sitting in lecture halls, staring at equations that refused to make sense, wondering how I had ended up there. I was desperately searching for some kind of meaning and purpose in the course I had chosen to study.

Now that I think about it, I wonder why, at such a young age, we are pressured into deciding what we want to "become." Back then, it felt like a single, irreversible choice that would define the rest of our lives. We were told to choose wisely, yet no one explained that choices could evolve —that the choice of a course of study was not static but could be adjusted to reflect one's development.

When I chose Economics, it wasn't love at first sight. It was a compromise after realizing I couldn't pursue my first choice, Law, at Covenant University. I had excelled in Economics during secondary school, so it seemed like a safe choice.

However, it wasn't long before I questioned my decision when the Advanced Maths came rolling in, and, because I wasn't mathematically inclined, I would spend long hours during the weekends struggling to grasp the concepts. This usually left me frustrated, crying, and wondering, *"Who sent me?"*[1] Why was I spending my life with so many numbers, when all I loved was reading books, building meaningful relationships, and teaching others?

This was my daily struggle until I was introduced to Development Economics (DE). This was a subject dedicated to the study of overcoming problems of extreme poverty and improving the quality of life.

As I delved deeper into DE, I began to find a sense of purpose in what I was studying and traced how it aligned with my natural interests. Growing up, I had idolized Mother Teresa; I would spend time reading about her and watching documentaries on her life. By studying about her, I learned the virtue of sacrificing momentary comfort to uphold the dignity of the people around me. Even before, I had always been drawn to causes that supported the poor and disadvantaged, so DE deeply resonated with me.

By my third year, I finally began to experience a sense of inner peace. Not because studying Economics had suddenly become easier, but because I'd finally found meaning in what I was doing.

---

1. Nigerian Pidgin used to express a rhetoric when one faces a challenging circumstance that makes one question their decision to do that thing in the first place.

While this might not be the case for everyone in their fields of study, I believe that at some point in life, whether inside or outside the four walls of a school, you will come to discover something that tugs at your heart and speaks to your natural interests.

For me, that moment in DE class marked the beginning of my journey.

Armed with a new sense of purpose, I became intentional about seeking out opportunities to evolve my passion for improving the lives of others, even after graduating with my degree in Economics.

While waiting to begin my National Youth Service Corps (NYSC)[2], I began volunteering full-time with a non-profit, Eagles Hope Foundation. I served in many capacities: HR, Learning and Development, Partnerships, and Fundraising.

Volunteering full-time meant learning to live on a small stipend and making sacrifices to ensure I showed up at my best each day. The best part, however, was that volunteering helped unravel, even more, the things that I was passionate about. The highlight of my time at Eagles Hope was the Summer Leadership Boot Camp for teenagers. Through that experience, I realized that my passion for economic development was really about shaping the lives of children and young adults.

During the camp, I discovered another piece
of myself. I found a person who was

---

2. A mandatory one-year national service placement for Nigerian university graduates.

willing to work beyond all limitations. I
found PURPOSE in the experience.

When NYSC began, I took a role as an HR intern in a tech consulting firm, but my heart was committed to the field of education. I was determined to keep finding ways to harness my passion for education and youth development. I served as Vice President of my education-focused Community Development Service (CDS) group, led workshops, and continued volunteering with Eagles Hope—facilitating leadership development workshops for secondary school students. Working with young people always stirred something in my heart because they gave me inspiration and hope for the kind of people they could grow to become.

One of the most memorable experiences of my NYSC year was building a school library for children near an Internally Displaced People's (IDP) camp. It had long been my dream to create a learning space where children could access books and study materials, and in God's way of connecting me to the people I needed to fulfil this dream, I met Chinenye Ezeakor during my NYSC. She shared a similar educational passion, and we set out to make this dream come true.

But passion alone wasn't enough.

The process of achieving this dream was where I truly began to understand what resilience meant. I also needed to have a fighting spirit, display a steady commitment, and work hard. These are values I would later learn are important to have, especially when embarking on the graduate application process.

As Chinenye and I continued to push towards our goal, we encountered our fair share of rejections. Potential funders turned us down, and even securing local authority approval for the library felt like a struggle. But we weren't ones to give up.

We continued to rework our project proposal until we got approval. When funds fell short, we developed innovative ways to finance the project—we engaged the community youths to paint the building, and enlisted local artisans for its renovation.

What had started as our vision soon became something every member of the community could proudly call their own. We reached out to bookstores, and some graciously offered us books at discounted prices. We also reached out to friends, family members, and colleagues; they supported the project in every way they could. There was no amount given that was considered too small towards the achievement of our goal. Every Naira mattered. We were proud to see our dream come true with the collective contribution from the local community.

The day the library opened, I watched children's faces break into wide smiles, delighted at the rows of books that were now theirs. Their laughter filled me with so much joy, and I knew I was exactly where I was meant to be. Looking back, the library project taught me some life lessons that would later become crucial in my graduate school journey.

First, when one door seems shut, there is always another way—even if it takes creativity, persistence, and a little extra faith. It might not be easy, but it is possible.

Second, never underestimate the power of community to make things happen. People can and will rally behind a vision they believe in. It was during this season that I truly understood the value of the relationships and support systems built over time.

Our fully stocked community library!

*Children from schools in the community, joyful after
visiting the library.*

As my NYSC year came to a close, it also signaled the end of my one-year job contract; it was time to begin thinking about my next steps. I was presented with the opportunity to continue at my placement firm in a full-time HR role, but I told my boss I would not be staying back. This came as a surprise to those around me because it was a good opportunity to start a corporate career with decent pay that afforded a good standard of living. Though I didn't know what the future held when I declined the offer to stay, I knew one thing: my life had found a purpose, and I couldn't settle for anything that didn't align with it.

It was from that moment that I decided to pursue a master's degree in Education.

> *Though I didn't know what the future held
> when I declined the offer to stay, I knew
> one thing: my life had found a purpose,
> and I couldn't settle for anything that
> didn't align with it.*

At first, my dreams were modest. I wasn't chasing the Ivy League or the world's best programs—just a good school in the UK. I wanted a smooth admission process and adequate funding. It was my first attempt at graduate applications, and I would have been content with any school that said, "Yes."

However, securing funding was challenging. Even though I secured admission from three different schools, I couldn't get the financial support I needed. I had my well-laid-out plans of going to graduate school right after my service year, and deferring was a delay I hadn't anticipated. I sought various opportunities to secure funding, but most of what I could get was either a partial scholarship or a 25% university tuition discount, which wasn't significant enough to cover my financial costs. After much of my efforts to secure full funding came to naught, it hit me that I wouldn't be leaving for school that year.

Letting go of the admission offers was painful, but after a while, I chose to look ahead at the other opportunities I had before me. I reminded myself that delay was not denial, and there were going to be other opportunities for me to try again to get what I wanted.

While waiting, I enrolled in a Postgraduate Diploma in Education (PGDE). That same year, 2017, I moved back to Lagos from Abuja, where I had just completed my NYSC. It wasn't long after my return that I came across the Teach For Nigeria (TFN) fellowship in my search for further development opportunities. This fellowship embodied the practical experience, values, and vision I had for my life. I remember the one line in their vision statement that prompted me to apply: *"I believe that one day every Nigerian child will have access to a quality education."* It was such a powerful vision, and I wanted to be a part of shaping that narrative.

I knew I had to apply.

When I remember the steps I took to be a part of this fellowship program, I am forever grateful I pressed on even when it seemed difficult. Joining Teach for Nigeria was a life-changing and unforgettable experience. I still cannot fathom how one event can forever transform the course of one's life.

In the weeks leading up to the TFN selection process, I fell sick twice and missed two selection task deadlines. The first task was a video submission, which I remember doing while recovering from malaria. The second task was to be an in-person assessment, but I missed that deadline, too.

When I realized I had again missed the due date for the second task, I was tempted to think that the opportunity was not for me. I was afraid to reach out to the recruitment team a second time to ask for another chance. It was my friend, Elda David, who dismissed my fears and pushed me to try one more time. *"Go in person,"* he said. *"The worst they can say is no."* Scared and uncertain, I walked into the TFN office, explained my situation to the HR lady, and to my surprise, was interviewed on the spot!

Now, imagine if I had gone unprepared. The saying, *"Success occurs when opportunity meets preparation,"* was true for me that day.

After the impromptu interview, I was graciously given another chance to proceed to the final stage of the selection process. I was so grateful and poured my best effort into preparing for the remaining stages.

A few weeks later, an email arrived bearing good news: I'd been selected as a part of the pioneer cohort of the Teach for Nigeria fellowship!

Dear Odinaka,

Congratulations!

We are delighted to officially welcome you as a **pioneer Fellow** to the 2017 Teach For Nigeria Fellowship.

This has been a very competitive selection process. Having received over 12,000 applications, our recruitment team including Teach For Nigeria Ambassadors, Board Members and External Assessors have assessed and selected a cohort that is nothing short of extraordinary, which is what you are! As a Teach For Nigeria Fellow, your commitment to take up the challenge to teach in an underserved school is invaluable.

As a Teach For Nigeria Fellow, your appointment will be effective for two years, starting from **July 11, 2017 until July 2019.** The Teach For Nigeria Fellowship is a full-time paid Fellowship program. You will receive a monthly stipend of 70, 000 naira, starting from September 2017.

My offer letter from the Teach for Nigeria fellowship.

All fellows were invited to an intensive six-week boot camp, after which we received our school postings. I was assigned to teach in Makoko, Lagos State. While I was aware that I had signed up to teach in underserved areas, I wasn't prepared to be sent to a place often described as the world's largest floating slum.

My first weeks in the classroom hit me with a flood of emotions. The stark reality of illiteracy and poverty among my pupils shook me to my core. I was assigned to teach a primary 5 (5th-grade) class of over 50 students, where only about a quarter of them could confidently read and write in English.

When I asked a question, only a few hands went up. Some children stared blankly at the board, trying to make sense of the words I'd written. A few could not even recognize the letters of the alphabet.

This situation left me with an internal battle and a multitude of questions. *How had these students progressed to primary 5 when so many struggled to grasp basic literacy skills?*

Unfortunately, it wasn't just the academic challenges that weighed on my heart; it was the lack of motivation to learn. I struggled to ignite that spark of curiosity in their eyes. Teaching a class that seemed disinterested in learning was emotionally draining.

Outside the classroom, things weren't any easier for my pupils. Many came to school without textbooks, pencils, or even breakfast. Some lived in homes that flooded when it rained; others shared cramped spaces with large families. Safety was never guaranteed, and the chaos of their environment often followed them into class. It became clear that learning was just one of the many battles they faced each day.

One day, as I stood there in front of the classroom, it hit me that my role was far deeper than simply delivering lessons. I was there to help them see what was possible, to offer hope where it often felt out of reach, and to create opportunities where there seemed to be none. I was not just their teacher; **I was their advocate for a better future.**

In environments like this, it can be easy to fall into the trap of thinking that one is a saviour with all the answers on hand. Thankfully, those six weeks of intensive training prepared me for the kind of leadership attitude that I needed to adapt to this kind of situation: one rooted in humility and collaboration. I'm grateful that those six weeks gave me the foundation I needed to think critically to solve the problems that were before me.

Beyond tackling literacy challenges, I knew I had to help my students see themselves differently. I needed to craft a vision that they could connect with and envision themselves being a part of. I knew they had to be on board with the vision; if not, no amount of teaching would make a difference. So I began working on their mindset. During our morning sessions, I would ask them questions like:

"How do you see yourself?"

"How do you see the possibilities that lie before you?"

"How can education be a game-changer for your present circumstances?"

I believe this was the hardest part of the work because after this was accomplished, learning became easier. My pupils would meet me after school with questions and a zeal to learn more. They also started seeing themselves differently

—as capable learners who could achieve anything they put their minds to.

Watching that transformation unfold was both rewarding and very emotional for me. I remember, vividly, the days I felt like quitting. I remember the days I felt so disappointed that the amount of work was not yielding the level of results I wanted to see. I remember falling sick on several occasions because the environment was unconducive and the work pressure was overwhelming.

Yet, this was what my pupils faced each day. Remembering that kept me going. So when I began to see small signs of growth—their improved reading, their confidence, their kindness towards one another it meant everything! The change didn't just show in their schoolwork; it also reflected in how they carried themselves, both in class and at home.

My students and I in the classroom.

If there was one thing they could attest to, and proudly told their friends in other classes, it was that *"Miss Ody cares about us; she loves us, and she wants us to be the best at whatever we do."* Hearing that always warmed my heart. Some days, I like to believe that the prayers and well-wishes of all my pupils paved the way for me in my graduate journey.

Even while doing the TFN fellowship, I had to carve out time each week to finish my teaching practice for my PGDE qualification. For two months, I spent about three hours a week teaching Commerce in a secondary school, also in Makoko. It was one of the most intense seasons of my life! I had never juggled so many responsibilities at once.

As the two-year Teach for Nigeria fellowship drew to a close, I knew it was time to give grad school another shot. I remember my close friend, Tobi, saying to me, *"It's time."* Unquestionably, I thought so too. However, my aspirations were different this time. If I were going to go to graduate school, it was going to be the best option out there.

And so the process began...

All through this journey, my parents questioned my decisions—and they weren't the only ones. Friends and well-meaning people often wondered if I was making the right choices. From the moment I chose to volunteer full-time with Eagles Hope Foundation after my BSc, to teaching in Makoko as a full-time teacher, which was the height of all they could take, my parents continued to question my ability to make wise decisions.

Eventually, my parents came to accept the path I had chosen—they didn't fully understand it, but they made peace with it. Much later, my father told me something interesting, he said that I reminded him of his father because of my passion for education. *Isn't it something—how acceptance does not always come at the beginning of a decision?* With time and experience, I've learned that once you find something that gives your life meaning, no amount of promised comfort, or even the doubts of those you love, can turn you away from it.

Hence:

> *You must always connect to purpose, what-*
> *ever venture you seek to take on in life,*
> *especially your graduate school journey.*
> *Purpose will always give you staying*
> *power when things get tough.*

Tip: If you haven't started, find ways to volunteer, intern, and participate in opportunities in your area of interest. These experiences will go a long way in boosting your application and will also help you discover other areas of specialization you might be interested in pursuing for your postgraduate study.

Chapter 2

The Application

Commit your works to the LORD [submit and trust them to Him], And your plans will succeed [if you respond to His will and guidance] (Proverbs 16:3, AMP).

The graduate process was meant to be easy—choose a school, apply, and get in, right? Far from it! The application process turned out to be one of the most testing seasons of my life. And a significant one at that—because the application process was only a glimpse of all the struggles, hard work, challenges, constraints, disappointments, and blessings too, that were to come in my graduate school journey.

At first, it seemed something was waiting to go wrong at every turn. It truly took the grace of God and the support of loved ones to keep me going.

To support you through this stage, I have included practical resources in what I call the Graduate Toolkit (included at the latter part of this book). It includes templates, check-lists, and tools drawn from my own journey to make your path a little smoother. Whenever you see a reference to the Toolkit, know that it is a resource created to help you navigate your own process intentionally.

Before I started applying to graduate school, I had specific criteria in mind. What helped the most was researching and noting each school's details against those criteria. (*You'll find a template in the Graduate Toolkit that you can easily format and personalize later to keep track of your applications so you don't miss any deadlines.*)

In 2019, this was the list I used to guide my search:

1. **Country:** I narrowed my search to three countries after considering factors like immigration laws and cost of living. Beyond that, I wanted to study in a place where I had some family support, offered a world-class education system, and provided strong post-graduate opportunities in my field.

For example, at the time of writing this, Canada offers clear pathways to Permanent Residency (PR) soon after graduation. The UK provides a two-year post-graduate work permit, though at a higher cost. The US typically offers a one-year post-study work permit, or two years for STEM degrees. In your own research, take note of such details for each country or school.

2. **Relevance of the program to your learning goal or interest:** I asked myself questions like, *Why am I doing this? How will this serve me in the future?* Having a clear "why" made it easier to choose programs I felt

passionate about, and that clarity strengthened my statement of purpose. It's always best to choose a program you're genuinely interested in. It makes the graduate journey much more fulfilling.

3. **Finance/Tuition:** Unless you have unlimited sponsorship, it's essential from day one to think carefully about tuition costs and funding options. For me, this was one of the biggest factors in my final decision. At the end of the day, it's the school you can afford that you'll attend.

4. **Entry requirements:** I made a list of commonly required documents—GRE, GMAT, IELTS/TOEFL, undergraduate transcripts, certificates, and recommendation letters. Knowing early what my program required (and the time and cost to prepare those materials) made a huge difference. Some programs demand standardized exams, so identifying these in advance helps you plan realistically.

5. **Duration of the program:** The duration of a program often affects its total cost and visa options. I noted how long each program lasted to compare which offered the best balance between time and outcome. In many cases, program length also influenced post-study work opportunities, making it another key factor to consider when applying.

These five factors provided a solid foundation for my graduate school search. You may find yourself adding other considerations that are unique to your situation, and that's perfectly okay. This stage takes time, which is why it helps to start early and plan intentionally. Knowing what you want will help you focus on what truly matters, and knowing your *why* will keep you steady when the process gets tough. For me, my final decision was ultimately shaped by two key things: the funding opportunities available and how well the program aligned with my long-term goals.

After narrowing down my options and finalizing my list of schools, I began working toward meeting the admission requirements.

At this point, I have to give a big shout-out to my friend, graduate school advisor, and CEO of Edwards Consulting, Bimpe Femi-Oyewo. While I was navigating this phase, Bimpe reached out and offered her consulting services, which included start-to-finish support for the entire graduate school application process. At the time, I could barely afford it, but she was patient with me, offering a generous discount and the flexibility of installment payments. Bimpe treated my application like it was her own, and every interaction reflected her belief in me and my potential to achieve my biggest dreams.

Having Bimpe by my side made a world of difference, and I remain deeply grateful for her support. That said, I also want you to know that working with a consultant is not the *only* path to success, especially if it's not within your means. With intentional research, community support, and a strong sense of purpose, there are many ways to navigate this process successfully.

What matters most is staying committed, resourceful, and trusting that with God's help, everything you need will come together.

. . .

Tip: My graduate school research sample:

University of Pennsylvania Graduate School of Education (GSE):

- **Major/Degree**: International Educational Development, Education Entrepreneurship, Education Policy.
- **Requirements**: Bachelor's degree, 1 personal statement, resume, 3 letters of recommendations, transcript, GRE, and TOEFL/IELTS.
- **Deadline**: Rolling basis. Application opens on September 1st, 2018. Priority submission is before March 1st, 2019.
- **Application fee:** The application fee ($75) is waived if the application is submitted before March 1st, 2019.
- **Links for General Information**: Info on International Educational Development, Info on Education Entrepreneurship, Info on Education Policy, and How to Apply.

Chapter 3

My Application Challenges

Behold, I am the LORD, the God of all flesh; is there anything too difficult for Me? (Jeremiah 32:27, AMP).

With my checklist in place, I began gathering the application requirements. Planning on paper was one thing; facing the reality of it all was another story entirely. This stage was far from easy, especially because it required heavy financial investment; talk about the plight of the Naira-Dollar exchange!

At the end of this chapter (*and in the Graduate Toolkit*), I've included a cost breakdown table and additional details on the expenses I incurred throughout the process.

At this point, I saw God come through for me financially like never before. It's easy to tell the story now in hindsight, but in those moments, it was a lot of learning to wait on God and trust in Him fully. And that, my friend, will *stretch* your faith!

The first thing I needed to do was book my IELTS and GRE dates. These are standard requirements for most schools in countries like the US, the UK, Canada, and Australia (*more details and study resources are in the Toolkit*).

The IELTS (International English Language Testing System) assesses English proficiency across four areas: Listening, Reading, Writing, and Speaking. The GRE (Graduate Record Examination) evaluates verbal and quantitative reasoning, analytical writing, and critical thinking. Both exams were required by the schools I planned to apply to. The minimum score varies across institutions, and this information is usually listed on each school's website.

I wanted to get these exams out of the way early, so I'd have my results ready before application deadlines. The only problem was that I couldn't afford either exam. Even if I pooled every kobo of my teaching stipend, it would still take months to save enough. This was only the beginning of the financial hurdles I would face in the application process.

I know many of us can relate to the heavy financial weight that comes with applying to graduate school abroad. I didn't know how I would pay the fee, but I trusted that a door would open. While hoping for a miracle, I decided to start studying for both exams and used every free IELTS practice resource I could find online.

Then it happened that, one day, a relative I hadn't spoken with in years visited. As he was leaving, he casually asked what I was up to. I told him about my graduate school plans, not expecting anything from the conversation. To my absolute surprise, he handed me an envelope with enough money to cover my IELTS fee. And just like that, provision came. I was so overwhelmed with joy. I registered immediately for the exam and picked the earliest available test date since I had already been preparing.

IELTS down, GRE to go.

Now, the GRE was more expensive than the IELTS, but the miracle of the first gave me faith that the fees would equally come through. True to my hope, one day while scrolling on Instagram, I stumbled on a $100 giveaway post by Mariam Olafuyi, CEO of GetIn Education Consulting. I needed more than that amount for my GRE, but I figured it was worth giving it a try.

The giveaway required an application process—yet another one I hadn't planned for. Applying was a bit daunting and time-consuming, but I needed the money. The fact that the provision had come as a gift the first time didn't mean it was going to happen the same way again. So, I set to work.

To my joy and delight, I was selected as one of the winners. Now I had the exam fee, but still needed to buy the GRE course materials.

At that moment, my mum stepped in. Seeing how committed I was to this process, she offered to pay for my study materials. She was a firm supporter of my dream to study abroad for my master's; she encouraged me, prayed with me, and stood in faith alongside me.

I was so excited that everything was coming together!

IELTS paid.

GRE paid.

Study materials covered.

Now it was time for the hard work to begin.

Balancing my full-time teaching job with studying for the GRE was no easy task. It was intense! I remember getting to school very early just so I could have some quiet time to study before my pupils arrived. During break times, while others relaxed or chatted, I'd be buried in GRE practice questions. And after school, when the last child had gone home, I'd stay behind to squeeze in more study time. My days were long and exhausting, but I had a short time to prepare for the exam, and I was determined to give it my best shot.

After weeks of pushing myself, the D-day finally came. The IELTS was a huge success, but I couldn't say the same for my GRE. One thing about the GRE is that you see your results the moment you finish. As soon as the screen blinked and my scores appeared, my heart sank. It wasn't terrible— just... *okay*. Average. A pass. I could have been excited, but I needed more than a pass to apply to an Ivy League school, which in this case was The University of Pennsylvania (UPenn). Aside from UPenn, I had to eliminate several other schools on my list, based on my GRE results.

As the reality sank in, I felt crushed. All those early mornings, sleepless nights, and sacrifices were gone, just like that. I cried so much that day. My friends and siblings tried to comfort me, reminding me that I had done my best, but it didn't matter to me. I felt like my best was not good enough.

I received suggestions to try applying to lower-ranking schools that might be easier to get into. But thinking about doing that made me even sadder. *If I was going to settle, why had I gone through all this stress from the beginning?*

During this time, my friend and advisor, Bimpe, did her best to encourage me. With her support, I kept applying to schools, including UPenn, while exploring other opportunities. Even though I felt discouraged, she believed that I still had what it took to impress the admissions committee. At a time when I didn't believe in myself because of an average result, it meant so much to have her believe that I had what it took.

Looking back, I'm so grateful for the hands that lifted me when I couldn't lift myself. Truly, when people say, *"It takes a village to send a child to school,"* I understand that saying with all my heart because it was my reality.

If you have never heard this before, I want you to hear it now: **I believe in you**. You have what it takes to accomplish your goals. Put in the work, put your hope and trust in God, and stay committed to the process.

Never give up.

I had people close to me who did not believe in my study-abroad dream. Some felt I was aiming too high. Others suggested that I apply to any random graduate entry programs or get a job rather than pursue my Ivy League dream.

My dad, whom I love dearly, as much as he wanted the best for me, was a very practical man who believed in *cutting his coat according to his size*. To him, it seemed more sensible to pursue a master's degree here in Nigeria, where the costs were within reach. He was even willing to support me financially if I took that path.

In fact, he went a step further by calling a few professors he knew at public universities, so I could speak with them to get more information about the requirements for their master's programs. He also encouraged me to apply to my alma mater, Covenant University. After all, it was a great school, and I had received an excellent undergraduate education there. His reasoning made sense—but that wasn't my dream.

I couldn't blame him for suggesting I focus on studying in the country. He didn't want to think of the financial burden of funding my master's education abroad or the possibility of being unable to meet all the costs.

In retrospect, I think deep down he believed I could achieve my dreams, but just wanted to stay practical. I assured him that I was going to get full funding. I am not even sure I fully believed it myself at the time, but I knew that I wasn't ready to back down just yet.

So, the journey continued.

I thought about re-taking the GRE, but I couldn't afford the fees, and there were no available dates that aligned with my timeline. So, rewriting was out of the question. I had no choice but to move forward with my application, trusting and believing that the other components would make up for where I was average. I decided to lean on the strength of my undergraduate transcript, statement of purpose, and leadership track record in the education field.

That weekend, I attended the Hallelujah festival, a praise and worship concert, and I prayed and danced my heart out. I poured everything before God. It was my way of releasing the tension and reminding myself that he had brought me this far for a reason.

Throughout the entire application process, my faith had never been stretched this much. Every stage came with its own set of challenges, each one testing my patience, endurance, and trust in God. But even in the moments when I felt worn out, I could sense his presence guiding me forward.

With the exams out of the way, the next time-sensitive task was getting my transcripts. Attending a private school, Covenant University, made the process of obtaining my transcript relatively smooth. I could simply request an electronic copy to be sent to my school of choice.

However, I also got to experience the other side of the coin when trying to obtain my PGDE transcript from the National Open University of Nigeria.

I had heard about transcript delays [and how challenging the process could be] from friends who attended public universities in Nigeria. I always listened with empathy, but having to navigate it myself gave me a firsthand understanding. The major hack in this process, whether you attended a public or private university, is to begin requesting your transcripts well ahead of time, at least 3–4 months before your application deadline, if possible.

You might be wondering why I needed my PGDE transcript when I already had one for my Bachelor's degree. The reason was simple: I wanted to strengthen my application for funding opportunities. Since my GRE score wasn't competitive enough for Ivy League programs, I decided to apply to schools that offered funding and didn't require the GRE.

One of those schools was George Washington University (GWU), which had numerous funding options for Education/International development, the very specialty I was interested in. I thought my PGDE would demonstrate my continued commitment to education, even though my undergraduate degree was in Economics.

If I had known how cumbersome the process would be, I would not have bothered! But these are the kinds of things you don't fully discover until you're deep into the process. Again, this is why it is so important to start early, to give yourself enough time to navigate unexpected delays and bottlenecks.

Unlike my undergraduate transcript, I had to go in person to the school to obtain my PGDE transcript and certificate. After paying the standard administrative fees, I was informed that it was *mandatory* to attend the graduation ceremony before I could receive my certificate. The graduation was in Abuja; I was in Lagos. I asked if I could collect it later at the Lagos office, but the answer was a firm no.

It was a ridiculous affair, to say the least.

Once again, I had to start gathering funds for an unplanned expense; this time, to travel for the graduation. It wasn't just money that was being spent; it was my time and energy, too.

I reached out to GWU, hoping they would accept my undergraduate transcript instead, but since I had already mentioned a second degree, they insisted on having that transcript. Talk about a perceived advantage turning into a disadvantage.

Though I was uncertain, it seemed like GWU was my best shot at securing funding with admission, so I decided to make the trip to Abuja.

I arrived for the graduation ceremony and afterward, proceeded to obtain my certificate. The process turned out to be a very disorganized one, and before we knew it, chaos had broken out. At some point, the officials announced that they would stop the distribution of the certificates due to the disorder. I couldn't believe my ears! *I had come this far, and I wasn't going to be able to get my certificate?*

To make matters worse, we were suddenly informed of a change in the clearance procedure to obtain our certificate. I tried making my way to the front of the queue and later to their office to speak to the staff, but I had no luck.

Later that evening, I had to reschedule my flight, seeing that the officers were hell-bent on not attending to any students. This, of course, was an additional, unplanned expense. After spending a few more days in Abuja, collection eventually resumed, and we were finally attended to. When it was my turn, I was told that my certificate was nowhere to be found. *"Can somebody please wake me up? This has to be a nightmare! So, where was the certificate then?"*

During the search, I was questioned by the staff as though I had been a ghost student, and it was my fault that my certificate had suddenly grown wings and disappeared. I asked if it could be reprinted, and they said it was not possible to do so at the time. Worse still, I was required to pay an additional fee just to open a case complaint for the missing certificate.

I eventually returned to Lagos without my certificate. When I followed up at the Lagos office, there was still no progress on their end.

At that point, I shared the challenges I had been facing with my parents, and my mom took it upon herself to escalate the issue. I am grateful for the kind of mother I have, especially in a country where following due process often leads to disappointment. Thankfully, after reaching out to several people, we were finally able to connect with someone who promised to follow up on the matter from Abuja. And you can imagine, we had to pay everyone we reached out to for their precious *time*.

Within a week, my certificate was miraculously found. But by then, it was too late to apply to GWU. While I could still be considered for admission, I had missed the scholarship deadlines. Also, my hard-earned application fee was gone, which was painful because every naira spent was valuable to me. In the end, because of the inefficiencies of the Nigerian public educational system, I had to forget about applying to that school.

Writing this part of the story gets me emotional, especially as I can still remember every detail of what it felt like at that moment. I had never felt so much despair. Initially, as I wrote this, I hesitated to go into the specifics of my transcript episode. But then I remembered the stories I'd heard from others who went through the same arduous process of securing their transcripts, and sometimes, like me, missed deadlines for valuable funding opportunities due to delays beyond their control. I decided that it was important to share my story, too. This particular experience made me understand how privilege and social background can sometimes influence the opportunities we have access to. At that moment, the Nigerian public education system failed me.

It's important to leave room for uncertainties when applying and to give yourself as much grace as possible for the things you can't control. Do your best, but recognize that, eventually, some things still fall to the level of the system you live in.

I didn't give up on my dream. I kept pushing because where there is a will, there is always a way. Getting this far simply meant I had to build greater tenacity if I was going to go further to achieve what I wanted. I was going to keep trying till there was nothing else I could do.

> *...eventually, some things still fall to the level*
> *of the system we live in.*

With GWU out of the way, I went back to the drawing board. By this time, my list of selected schools was growing smaller. Only two remained: New York University (NYU) and the University of North Carolina (UNC). I'm not sure why, but I decided to keep trying UPenn. At that point, I realized the worst that could happen was a *"Sorry, you are not qualified."* But at least I'd know I gave it my all.

I must confess, I was tired, drained, and emotionally overwhelmed. Spending weeks crafting essays for my GWU scholarship applications, only to discard the process, was painful. But there was no time to dwell on it for long; I had to forge ahead with the remaining schools on my list.

I applied to NYU, UNC, and finally UPenn. Unlike the UK, most US schools require that you submit a transcript evaluation along with your transcripts. This is usually done if you were schooled outside of the US. It is a process to help compare your academic records with the US equivalent. (*In the Graduate Toolkit, you'll find a step-by-step guide to completing your transcript evaluation for US schools.*)

This, of course, was another costly process.

At this stage in the process, I had exhausted all my financial resources. In applying to schools, I had written numerous emails requesting application fee waivers—anything to reduce the costs of the already expensive process. It was then that I discovered that for some schools, I could also request a waiver for the IELTS requirement. All I needed was an official letter from my undergraduate institution, confirming that English was the language of instruction.

These are the kinds of hacks that you can try when applying to schools. I learned about the IELTS waiver at a time when I was completely drained financially. After paying to write the IELTS, I was shocked to find out I would still need to pay additional fees to send my results to each school. *What?!* Once I learned that, I became more intentional about seeking out waivers to reduce the number of schools I'd need to send my IELTS results to.

Meanwhile, I needed to begin my transcript evaluation

process as soon as possible since time was running out. But I hesitated, because I couldn't afford it just yet. I had already cut my living expenses, but I still had a long way to go.

In that season, I remain ever so grateful for all the people who showed up in every way they could.

During this time, my favorite song was *Waymaker* by Sinach. That song was constantly on repeat! I just needed to believe that somehow God would come through for me amidst everything I was facing.

It was 24 hours before the deadline, and I still couldn't pay the transcript evaluation fee. I was emotionally exhausted and didn't know who to turn to. I didn't even try to borrow money because I knew my teacher's stipend wouldn't allow me to repay it.

That night, I went to bed in tears, exhausted, and wondering if this was to be the end of my journey. I just couldn't see a way forward.

The lyrics of *Waymaker* were all I could hold on to:

"Way maker,
Miracle worker,
Promise keeper,
Light in the darkness.
My God, that is who You are...
Even when I don't see it, You're working.
Even when I don't feel it, You're working.
You never stop, You never stop working."

That was probably the longest night of my life, and there were still many more hurdles ahead.

The next morning, I woke up as usual, getting ready to head to school and meet my students. Then my sister,

Onyinye, walked into the room. I will never forget what she said: *"Ody, I wish I had the money to sponsor the entire process, and I even wish I had the money you needed right now. But my husband and I have been talking, and we have decided to withdraw from our mutual funds to complete whatever amount is left for the transcript evaluation."*

I was in shock and broke down crying. How God kept coming through for me every single time was *absolutely* mind-blowing. These moments continued to strengthen my faith on the journey, reminding me that God was with me and He would never let me down.

It's hard to think back on this journey and not be overwhelmed with gratitude for all the miracles and all the people God used to sponsor the process.

Once again, the finances came through, and I was ready to continue. The very same day I received the money, I applied for the processing of my transcript evaluation. While that was underway, I began sharing my Statement of Purpose (SOP)—as well as my personal statement—with a few trusted friends and mentors for review. I made sure to do this early, about four to six weeks before the deadline, so they would have enough time to read through it carefully and offer meaningful feedback.

I deliberately chose just a handful of people to share this with—especially those who had prior experience reviewing graduate school essays—because I didn't want to get caught in the confusion and overwhelm that often come with too many opinions.

The Statement of Purpose is your opportunity to tell your story. It's the part of your application that truly sets you apart. It's a chance to show the committee your competence, qualifications, and passion for your chosen field. It's also where you address any gaps in your application and explain why you're a strong fit for your chosen program.

The importance of your statement cannot be overemphasized. That's why I've included a dedicated section in the Graduate Toolkit to guide you through the process of writing a strong and compelling statement.

Shout-out again to Bimpe, and especially to Henry, my life partner, who had my back through it all. I had the full support of my friends and mentors; if they weren't praying for me or contributing to my application fees, they were reviewing my essays and writing recommendations. In every way they could help, they showed up, constantly being a source of encouragement.

Of course, there were a few people who thought I was doing too much, but thankfully, the voices of the encouragers were louder than those of the naysayers. More importantly, this was something I deeply wanted for myself. I had a vision and a goal for graduate school abroad, and I was not going to relent till I achieved it.

By this point, I was gradually checking off all my application requirements—by the way, I've included this same checklist in the Toolkit. The last major hurdle was securing my letters of reference. I needed about three to four, depending on the school, and while it wasn't compulsory, it was strongly recommended to include at least one from a professor.

I began reaching out to my undergraduate supervisor and two other professors to request reference letters. I felt it would be better to go in person to make this request, knowing that contacting my undergraduate supervisor via email could be difficult. So, I made the trip from Lagos to Ota, Ogun State. I initially planned to return the same day, hoping that a few hours would be enough to sort everything out. But as it turned out, it wasn't. I ended up staying back to ensure I had everything sorted out. Once I had the assurance that it was all in place, I returned home.

Next, I had to finalize my personal statements and any scholarship essays I needed to submit. Two days before the UPenn deadline, I received an email notification that one of my referees had yet to complete their submission. I was shocked! I thought everything had been sorted. I began frantically calling, texting, and emailing my supervisor...no response. I reached out to a friend in school, who mentioned she hadn't seen him on campus and had gone to his office several times with no luck.

This was another epic moment when I broke down in tears. *How could this be happening at the last minute?* Who would I reach out to for a reference 24 hours before the deadline? Everyone else I could ask had already been listed as secondary referees.

To this day, I bless God for my friend, Chisom. She made every effort to find someone who could stand in for me at the last minute. My dear friend went to the office of one of our most senior professors, pleading for his help, and waited patiently, even with all the challenges involved in notifying the school of a last-minute referee change.

Naturally, the professor wasn't too pleased with the request, which he considered irresponsible given the late notice, but my friend was not one to give up. Thankfully, he agreed to assist, and she stayed back in the office to ensure everything was properly written, reviewed, stamped, and uploaded. My gosh! The beauty of friendships! I thank God for the friends he has blessed me with.

You cannot do life alone, and this was a prime example.

That moment taught me a very powerful lesson about friendships. Friends who believe in your vision, friends who have your back, friends who will fight for you and do everything to make you succeed...they are must-haves.

With that, I was done with submitting all the requirements. Or so I thought.

Breakdown of major costs incurred in my application process in 2019

Budget Plan
Cost
IELTS: $255
GRE: $220
Application Fee (per school): $100
WES Transcript Evaluation: $217
Visa Application: $160
SEVIS Fee: $350
Total: $1302

Note: Please keep in mind that the financial breakdown I've shared does not capture every cost I incurred along the way. Additional administrative and logistical expenses—like flying from Lagos to Abuja for my visa interview, extra fees from fluctuating exchange rates, and payments to an education consultant who helped me identify scholarship opportunities —added up as well.

Chapter 4

Securing Financial Opportunities for Graduate School

Let us hold tightly without wavering to the hope we affirm, for God can be trusted to keep his promise (Hebrews 10:23, NLT).

I f I were to rank the questions I am constantly asked about graduate school, securing scholarships would easily make the top 3 on the list. And why not? It makes perfect sense that funding is an utmost concern in the minds of people seeking graduate studies abroad.

When it comes to securing financial opportunities to study, the most popular pathway is getting a scholarship. However, with the increasing number of people applying to graduate schools abroad, scholarships have become more competitive. If this is a path you're considering, it is important to realize that the scholarship preparation begins way before the admission cycle. In other words, you need to begin building a track record as soon as possible to convince the scholarship committee that you deserve a scholarship.

If you haven't started, it's not too late. Start affiliating yourself with groups that have a track record of doing good in their communities. Other pathways to consider for funding opportunities include Graduate Assistantships/Research Assistantships, Government funding, Multilateral Funding, Fellowships, etc. To find these opportunities, I dd a lot of research on the university websites, common scholarship forums, related websites, and got the help of an educational consultant.

> *It is important to realize that the scholarship preparation begins way before the admission cycle. In other words, you want to begin building a track record as soon as possible to convince the scholarship committee that you deserve a scholarship.*

My funding journey was a mix of fellowships and scholarships. These came as a result of learning to craft my story, hard work, and, of course, grace. Securing funding, though not as rigorous as the admission process, is a story worth telling.

After I had successfully managed to submit my application materials, I started preparing my scholarship essay. I was particularly interested in the funding opportunity at UPenn because it awarded a full tuition PennUNESCO Scholarship worth over $70,000 at the time. Though daunting, it was worth trying.

I submitted my essay for the application just before the deadline. Then on the day of the deadline, something unusual happened. I can't fully explain it or recall every detail, but I had a strong, instinctive urge to email the scholarship committee to confirm they had received my application. I did this because after sending my application, I had not received any notification or confirmation email as proof that I had successfully submitted it. Technically, it should not have been a big deal because I was sure I submitted it. But still, I decided to check.

I sent an email and thankfully, received a response almost immediately. To my dismay, the lady on the other end replied that there was no record of my submission in their system. I was shocked!

A flood of thoughts ran through my mind:

What if I hadn't emailed to confirm?

What if they had responded when it was too late?

I was so thankful for the time difference because that bought me a few hours before the deadline.

The disheartening part of this incident was that I had not saved my essay anywhere. No backup. That moment taught me a valuable lesson: to always keep copies of my application materials. Not only can this be a great save in emergencies, but backups can also serve as useful resources for future applications.

Tip: Always have backups of your application materials. Save them in multiple places. They can be reused, repurposed, and might just save you from a crisis.

In my case, I had typed my essay directly into the application portal. So, when I realized I had to write from scratch again, I began to panic.

What if I don't make a good submission like the first draft?

But I did not even have the time to second-guess myself. I had to start writing immediately.

I messaged my partner, Henry, and told him what was going on. He said to me, *"Babe, just write. Write from your heart, and when you are done, send it to me on WhatsApp. We will see how we can edit it."* Once again, I was reminded of the gift of wonderful relationships and the support system God had placed around me.

I began writing, and when I was done, I sent it to him so we could edit it together. I submitted just an hour before the deadline.

Whew!

Having done my part, all that was left to do was to pray. And boy, did I pray hard! I cannot remember ever praying as hard as I did during that period.

You'd think I'd feel relieved that the entire application was over, but instead, a wave of restlessness descended on me. Waiting [or having to deal with uncertainties] has never been my strong suit, yet life demands that we grow that muscle of patience. What made the waiting even harder was knowing that the scholarship would be awarded to only two people. Just two. I didn't even want to begin imagining the caliber of applicants I was up against, especially for an Ivy League school.

I also applied to the P.E.O. International Peace Fellowship, a scholarship dedicated to supporting women using their education to make a positive impact in the world. Thanks to Bimpe of Edward Consulting, who had also been a 2-time recipient of this award, I was able to put in a stellar application. Even though I was hoping for the full tuition PennUNESCO scholarship, I would still need additional funding to cover my living expenses. So, I had to apply for other scholarships.

One of the biggest tips I can offer concerning scholarship applications is to master the art of storytelling; it will make all the difference in your application. Storytelling is not about fabricating lies or exaggerating your experiences; it is about sharing your story with authenticity and vulnerability. And vulnerability does not mean seeking pity for your circumstances; rather, it involves demonstrating strength, purpose, value, and tenacity even in the face of odds.

I hope you remember this when applying.

> *Learn the art of storytelling. It will make a huge difference in your application. Remember, storytelling is not about exaggerations or fabricating lies; it is about sharing your story with authenticity and vulnerability.*

Chapter 5

The Wait: A Process We All Experience

And we know that God causes everything to work together for the good of those who love God and are called according to his purpose for them (Romans 8:28, NLT).

I f you thought the scholarship application process was tough, the waiting period was a whole *'nother* battle. It was tough! But here's the beauty of the waiting period in any situation: it teaches you patience and trust in God's timing. And when everything finally comes together, you'll look back and realize that God was always in the details, walking with you every step of the way.

At some point, I had to distract myself from the anxiety of waiting. The uncertainty was killing me. The what-ifs were scary. I had done my all, and really, all I could do was leave it in the hands of God. I wish I could find the right words to fully describe how scary the wait was! I felt emotions that I had never felt before, and it was only by God's grace that I got through that phase.

A few months later, the results started to arrive. I had

been admitted to New York University. I was so happy. At least it gave me some hope. Maybe, just maybe, UPenn would find me worthy of admission, too.

I called my siblings and my mum immediately to share the good news, and they were all so happy for me. But then came the next, most important question: "*Did you get a scholarship too?*" In all my excitement, I had not even checked. So I scrolled to the end of the letter...no scholarship. *This has to be a joke, hahaha.* There had to be some sort of stipend somewhere.

I messaged Bimpe expressing my dismay, and she advised that I email the school asking if they had internal funding opportunities available. We sat down to craft the email together and sent it immediately. Shortly after, they responded that there was no funding available for international students. I was stunned. *How can you promote diversity and encourage international students to attend your institution in New York, yet offer no form of funding for International students?* It felt contradictory. I knew, without a doubt, that I would not be accepting the offer.

My dear mum was so concerned when she saw how disappointed I was. She started suggesting ways to help, whether by taking a loan or contributing in any way she could. But I told her not to worry. To be honest, I was also put off by the school's lack of funding options.

Slowly, responses from other institutions began to come in. Only UPenn maintained radio silence. I hadn't heard a word.

They had mentioned I was going to hear back in a few weeks, but months had passed without an update. I became frantic with worry. Perhaps I did not make it. I just did not know.

I thank God for my friends who kept me sane during the waiting. I remember a particular conversation with someone who had gotten admission to another elite school in the US. He mentioned that his admission came within a short time and speculated that perhaps I had been placed on a waitlist, which could explain why I hadn't heard back yet.

His narrative did not sit well with me. It made me scared because if I was on the waitlist, there was a probability I might not get in unless someone else dropped off. And that also depended on the number of people on the waitlist. Thankfully, for every narrative that brought fear, I had a thousand reassuring words from my partner, loved ones, family, and friends.

That very night, after the conversation with this guy, I couldn't sleep. I was up thinking and praying until I finally drifted off. I remember waking up at 4 AM to use the restroom, and I picked up my phone to randomly check my email. Checking my email first thing when I woke up had fast become a habit in my graduate process. In this graduate application journey, checking your email regularly is very important.

Tip: Never go more than two days without checking your email. And always keep an eye on your spam or junk folders because sometimes an important email may find its way to such folders.

That fateful morning, I saw the email I had been waiting for. Only that this time, instead of congratulations, it read:

Admission Decision Now Available
1 message

Penn GSE Graduate Admissions <admissions@gse.upenn.edu>   Wed, Apr 24, 2019 at 1:52 AM
Reply-To: Penn GSE Admissions and Financial Aid <admissions@gse.upenn.edu>
To: chukwuodinakauzoma@gmail.com

April 23, 2019

Dear Odinaka,

Thank you for your application to the University of Pennsylvania Graduate School of Education (Penn GSE). The faculty has reviewed your application carefully and made an admission decision on your file. Your admission decision is now available online.

You can access your decision by logging into your online application account. Please note that hard copy letters will not be mailed. Thank you for your interest in pursuing graduate studies at Penn GSE.

My admission decision from UPenn.

Why couldn't they just make this easier for me? My hands were shaking. My heart was beating so fast.

I tried to calm myself. Even though I told myself that it was not the end of the world, it felt like it was. I shakily opened my dashboard to download the letter, and what I saw next blew my mind.

April 23, 2019

Dear Odinaka,

Congratulations! The faculty is pleased to offer you Fall 2019 admission to the University of Pennsylvania Graduate School of Education (Penn GSE) International Educational Development, MSEd program. In addition, we're delighted to be able to offer you $13,500 in merit scholarship to help you achieve your academic goals.

We chose this year's class from an exceptional applicant pool whose abilities, talents, and research interests will enrich your experience. The faculty is impressed by your achievements and promise and looks forward to the contributions you will make as a member of our dynamic community. Should you accept our offer, you will join a talented group of students also selected from a superbly accomplished pool of candidates who presented highly competitive, deserving and compelling cases for admission.

Successful Penn GSE students will also take their place among a powerful and highly regarded alumni network comprised of practitioner-scholars who occupy leadership positions in higher education, government, nonprofits, and industry. We are confident that your time at Penn GSE will be challenging and rewarding. Kindly respond to this offer of admission by completing the decision form (available from your status page). Please also email the following page as an attachment to admissions@gse.upenn.edu after you print, complete and scan the document.

If you do not accept, we want to be able to extend this offer to another student. Scholarships are highly competitive and can only be guaranteed until April 15 the date until which the Council of Graduate Schools agreement resolution allows you to make a decision. The April 15 common reply date is for all applicants admitted through March 15. Applicants admitted on or after March 16 have 30 days from the date of this letter to reply.

This offer of admission is contingent upon receipt of official transcripts from all colleges and universities attended within the United States. If you have attended college or university outside of the United States, a course-by-course evaluation from a NACES member is required. If you are currently enrolled in a degree program, please note this offer of admission is contingent upon your successful completion of that program. You cannot begin a graduate program at Penn GSE until official notification of your baccalaureate degree conferral has been received.

My letter of admission from UPenn!

Not only had I been offered admission, but I was also given a merit scholarship. I began crying so hard. There I was thinking that I was on the waitlist because I wasn't good enough due to my GRE score. Yet here I was, being offered a merit scholarship!

I could not wait for my parents to wake up. The moment they did, I ran to their room to tell them the good news. My mum was overjoyed. My dad is not the overly expressive type, but I could see him beaming with pride! My heart was full of so much joy. I had brought that *look* to my dad's face. Wow! Their daughter was going to an Ivy League school!

Next, the major question popped up about whether there was any funding. I mentioned I had been awarded a $13,500 merit scholarship. Of course, that wasn't a significant enough figure for the tuition. But being awarded a merit scholarship boosted my confidence in the quality of my application. However, that did not solve the financial challenge for my parents.

My dad, ever the practical man, said his congratulations, asked how much the tuition was in Naira, and replied, *"Wow, that is expensive,"* when I told him. It looked like a tricky situation. But my mum said, *"If God has brought her this far, let's thank Him, celebrate, and trust Him to provide all she needs,"* and that's exactly what I did. I needed to at least pause and thank God. Too often in life, we get so caught up worrying about the *next thing* that we forget to thank God for the miracles we currently live in.

And you know what? That very day, I received an email from P.E.O. confirming that I had been awarded the IPS scholarship, valued at $12,500! There was so much excitement and heartfelt thanks in one day. My mother was so happy! Of course, she reminded my father of her words earlier that morning. By then, everyone had come to believe that God truly had a plan here. And as He had begun my journey, He would perfect it.

We now had $26,000, and needed $46,000 more to cover the tuition. It wasn't the figures that made me hopeful;

it was seeing God come through for me repeatedly that strengthened my faith in the knowledge that the $46,000 would also come through. At this point, the biggest game-changer would be receiving the full-tuition PennUNESCO scholarship.

And so the waiting continued.

I had assumed the UNESCO scholarship decision was going to be announced alongside the admission offer, but since I had gotten no notification, I kept waiting. After a few weeks, my patience began to fray. *If I have not been selected, I should at least get a rejection email, so I know my next step, right?*

I started to get anxious again. Knowing that it was only two people who were awarded each year didn't help. Neither did it help to remember that no Nigerian had received the scholarship in the past. But I had no option but to just keep hoping for the best.

As always, my support system was there to cheer me on and encourage me. A special mention to my dear friend, late Titilade Raji; *I will always remember your love and unwavering support during that period.* Titi was my teaching partner during the TFN fellowship, and she did everything she could to support me, even as I tried to balance the demands of teaching with the intensity of applying to graduate school. *Titi, I love and miss you dearly.*

It had now been three weeks since my admission offer, and I still did not have an update about my scholarship status. Bimpe and Henry both suggested I send a follow-up email to the admissions committee to check on the status of my application. I'd learned to communicate strategically in emails, so I took care not to sound anxious or desperate.

Unlike previous instances when responses were prompt, this time I received nothing.

With that, I decided to take a hands-off approach for a while and focus on other things in my life. Though if I'm being honest, I wasn't very successful at that. Even during my breaks at school, I would hop on a bike to the nearest chapel to meditate and pray.

On one of those days, Titi suggested we go watch a movie because I needed the distraction. So, we set out to see one of the Marvel movies that had just been released. At least, it was something exciting to do.

By the time we got to the cinema, we realized we had mixed up the show times, and there were no more screenings for the day. So we went outside, debating whether to head home or find something else to do. I mentioned to Titi that I would probably head to the chapel first before going home. Just as we were talking, I received an email alert.

It was from the scholarship committee, and it read:

Dear Odinaka,

I am very pleased to report that you will be offered the Penn-UNESCO Fellowship for study in IEDP at Penn this coming academic year, beginning in late August 2019. Your strong record of accomplishments and commitment to the field of education was persuasive to the Penn GSE administration and to us in IEDP. Congratulations!

The formal award letter (with full details) will be sent to you very soon by PennGSE.

We very much hope that you will be able to join us, and would like to hear from you NO LATER than one week from today if you plan to accept this award. I should also add that I expect to be your faculty Advisor, and I will have some UNESCO Chair-related voluntary responsibilities for you over the academic year.

We suggest that you begin to make preparations for coming to join an excellent group of global Masters students. We look forward very much to your studying with us at Penn.

Best Wishes,

My offer of the UNESCO Fellow Award for PennGSE IEDP.

I was awarded the Penn UNESCO scholarship! I broke down right there in public. I started screaming and crying outside the cinema. Passers-by thought something terrible had happened, and Titi had to explain to them that I was just overwhelmed with joy. That feeling will probably never leave me. Titi and I kept rejoicing, and then I started making calls to everyone who had been praying and supporting me on the journey. It was so surreal! I called my parents, and I could hear my mum say to my dad, *"You see, God has done it!"* We were all so happy. One good news wiped away all the tears of the past. It was refreshing news.

The second part of this story is just ahead. But before we continue, I invite you to pause and reflect on your story, and the thread of hope that runs through it. Even as I write this, I am reminded that just one *yes* can wipe away all your tears of pain. To get that one yes, you cannot give up because of the nos.

> *Sometimes all it takes is one yes to wipe away*
> *years of tears. And to get that one yes, you*
> *cannot give up because of the nos.*

To get to that *yes*, you have to keep trying, believing, hoping, praying, and working toward what you want. And when you find it hard to believe, surround yourself with people who believe; people who remind you of your worth, and people who will continue to have faith even when yours falters.

People are a very important part of your journey. Life is much easier when you are surrounded by the right people. In addition, don't only seek to be surrounded by the right people, but also try to be that friend who lifts others when they need it most.

Chapter 6

Another Prayer Point: The Visa Application

And I am certain that God, who began the good work within you, will continue his work until it is finally finished on the day when Christ Jesus returns. (Philippians 1:6, NLT).

The visa application process was the final phase I needed to complete to seal the deal. Anybody who has gone through the US visa application process knows it is a prayer point by itself. (*In the Toolkit, you will find crucial tips and step-by-step guidance to help you prepare effectively for your visa interview. These resources are designed to make the process less stressful, so you can approach it with confidence and clarity.*)

With all my tuition and living expenses covered through scholarships and financial support statements from my parents, I felt more confident about my visa application. I set out to book an interview appointment, only to discover there were no dates available. The earliest slot was going to be in the month of my school resumption. I didn't know what to think or do. My sister, Adaeze, encouraged me to keep checking every day.

I reached out to a friend who had already booked his appointment for some help. He explained that during peak periods, there is often a shortage of visa slots because so many people are applying at the same time. He also advised that I keep checking back every day in case a slot opened up. Eventually, one did, and it was in Abuja. I could not even complain; I was just grateful to have found a date. I quickly gathered my documents, had a mock interview with Bimpe, and set out for Abuja.

On the day of the interview, I was incredibly nervous, mostly because of the stories I had heard about visa rejections. As I waited in the queue, I watched the reactions of people ahead of me leaving their appointments. Some looked disappointed, some seemed hopeful, and some were jubilating. It felt like watching a movie in real time. All I could do was trust that the God who had brought me this far would see me through.

Finally, it was my turn. I summoned up confidence and walked up to my booth. The officer asked questions based on the details I had provided in my visa application. The conversation shifted, and he focused more on the financial aspect of my funding. To my surprise, he seemed to have some doubts about my funding sources. Perhaps he needed to verify that it was legitimate because he kept pressing in with more questions. At the end of the interview, he handed me a slip and, apologetically, said that he couldn't issue my visa just yet. They needed to further evaluate my documents before making a final decision.

I did not know how to feel at that point. I was in limbo. It wasn't a yes or a no, and I was not given a timeline for the final decision. I just had to wait patiently. I stayed back in Abuja for two days, hoping for some news. When nothing came, I made arrangements to return to Lagos. Then, on the very day I was meant to leave, I received an email: the evaluation had been successful, and my visa was ready for pick up.

My joy knew no bounds.

I picked up my passport with my visa inside. I was teary-eyed. The first part of my graduate journey had finally come to an end. Seven months of hard work, perseverance, tenacity, and resilience were over. Tears of joy and gratitude flowed freely.

With my visa in my hands, it finally felt real. UPenn wasn't just a dream anymore. It was happening. Graduate school, UPenn, here I come!

At that moment, I allowed myself to take it all in.

The first part of the journey was complete. The applications, the waiting, the prayers, the unexpected turns; all of it had led here. I had gotten the admission, the scholarships, and the visa. Now, a new season was about to begin.

Getting in was one thing; navigating the life that came after was a different experience altogether. I wish I could say I was fully prepared for the journey, but the truth is, it was only the beginning of a much bigger process.

But hey, don't worry, it wasn't all gloom. It just required some adjustment... and a whole lot more grace.

In Part Two, I'll share what life in graduate school looked like: the joys, the tensions, the cultural shifts, and everything in between. Your story may not look exactly like mine, but I have no doubt parts of it will feel familiar.

Part Two

So You Got Into Grad School... What next?

Introduction: The Life of a Graduate Student

Getting into graduate school was only the beginning of what was to be a long journey of ups, downs, highs, and lows. It was laced with a lot of excitement, anxiety, and learning curves all at the same time.

This is my story.

Yes, I finally got into graduate school—into one of the best colleges in the US! My joy knew no bounds, and I could hardly wrap my mind around the weight of the opportunities ahead of me.

For the first time in my life, I was leaving home for another continent to begin an entirely new chapter. I remember sitting on the plane, unable to put my feelings into words.

Was it anxiety?

Was it joy?

Was it the ache of missing my loved ones?

Or the excitement of stepping into something new?

At that point, I had to accept that it was okay to feel

everything at once. It was okay to sit with a mix of emotions. It was all part of the process.

Perhaps what made it easier for me was knowing I had a sister, Nneka, who already lived in the US and had some experience with relocating. Her journey had been for professional reasons, not academic ones, but it was still comforting to know I was not completely alone.

As you read, I hope you'll realize that you're not alone either. Many others have walked this path you're about to begin.

Chapter 7

Welcome to Another Man's Land

*Indeed, the LORD is the one who will keep on walking in
front of you. He'll be with you and won't leave you or abandon
you, so never be afraid and never be dismayed.*
(Deuteronomy 31:8, ISV)

The week finally arrived for my departure to the US.
I wasn't sure how time had passed so quickly,
but somehow, July was coming to an end, and I was
scheduled to travel in less than a week. Most US schools
resume for the fall semester in August, and I had planned to
arrive a few days early to settle in before classes began. I was
relieved when my visa got approved just in time. It eased my
anxieties about the possibility of resuming school later than
planned.

Normally, it is advised that you wait until your visa is
approved before booking your flight, but I booked mine early
—in faith—because I couldn't bear the thought of inflated

ticket prices if I waited too long. I wouldn't exactly recommend my approach, but it worked in my favor, and honestly, I was so grateful it did!

Getting ready to travel for school came with a flood of emotions. There was the anxiety of what lay ahead, especially knowing that I was leaving home behind and would be living miles away from my family and friends.

In the days leading up to my departure, friends and loved ones came by to visit, and their presence left me feeling emotional. Those moments were bittersweet—on one hand, we were happy that I was finally going abroad to pursue a long-time dream, but on the other hand, I knew I would miss them beyond words. I couldn't help wondering if things would remain the same after I was gone.

There was also the anxiety of making sure I was fully prepared for the move. There were several important things I had to put in place to ensure everything was set for my departure and arrival in the US. I have shared these things in what I call the *30-minute settling manual* in the Toolkit.

Here, I must give honor to whom honor is due—my mum did the most before I traveled! She filled my luggage with foodstuffs, picked out Ankara clothing that later became my little connection to home, and handled many other details I hadn't even thought about. I couldn't thank her enough; I still can't. Every step of the way, she was there encouraging me, praying for me, and giving to me.

My travel day was an emotional one. I was excited right up until it was time for the goodbye hugs. I hugged my dad tightly, knowing I would miss him so much. I would miss waking up to his quiet, gentle smile as he ate breakfast in the dining room. I would miss simply having him around. I was going to miss my mum too, but I knew she was going to visit me at some point, and that gave me some comfort.

I was also going to be living apart from my brother, with whom I had shared most of my growing-up days. And then there was my sister, Onyinye, who had held me up throughout this journey. Her home had been a haven for me during the hard days of pursuing the teaching fellowship, completing my application, and navigating the tension and anxiety that came with it. She supported me in every way she could: through her words, her prayers, and even her finances. I was also going to miss my nephew, Jasper, whom I'd grown so fond of as I had co-nurtured him from infancy.

The hardest part was the thought of starting a long-distance relationship with my boyfriend; *when next would we have a physical date?*

I could go on listing all the people I knew I'd miss and what that meant for me. But the point is this: relocation, as exciting as it is, often comes with real physical and emotional effects. It takes strength to go through those first days of being away from home, far from everything you've ever known and from the people you love. [1] [2]

Choosing to relocate is an act of bravery and courage. It's also a journey of faith, because it's not a step you take unless you truly believe that something better lies ahead.

My arrival in the US was smooth because one of my sisters, Nneka, lived there with her family. At this point, I think it's important to break down my family tree. I come from a family of seven—my mum, dad, four girls, and one boy. I'm the fourth girl. Throughout my story, you'll see the different ways my siblings supported me and held me up during various phases of my graduate school journey.

Nneka was there to welcome me into her home in

Wisconsin. I spent a week with her before heading to my school in Philadelphia. That week became one of my fondest memories from my first days. In those moments, I came to cherish family more and truly understand what it meant to be surrounded by such a measure of love.

If you're reading this and thinking, *"But I don't have anyone in the US,"* please don't be discouraged. While I was lucky to have the gift of my sister's presence, many others have successfully built a community from scratch. You can start by reaching out to current students at your school, especially those from your home country or continent. Join WhatsApp or Facebook groups for international students, African students, or specific interest groups. Your people are out there. Community can be built, even if it doesn't begin with family. The key is to stay open, reach out, and let others in. You don't have to do this journey alone—and you shouldn't, if you can help it.

At my sister's house, I picked up my search for graduate student jobs again. I had started searching before leaving Nigeria, but with so many other things demanding my attention, I couldn't give it my full focus. With a bit more breathing space, I continued the search and came across a Graduate Assistant position at my school's tutoring center.

With my background and passion for education, I had a strong feeling I would love the role even before reading the job description. And when I did read it, it felt like a perfect fit. The institution was a center that placed students at the heart of everything it did, ensuring they received the support they needed to excel academically. That mission deeply resonated with me.

Although it wasn't a teaching role and I would be coordinating the student tutors who provided the service, I applied anyway. It wasn't long before I received an email inviting me to an interview the following week. I was overwhelmed with joy! It was the first application I had submitted, and to get such a prompt response felt incredible. I let them know the date I'd be arriving on campus, and the interview was scheduled for that same week.

Before I knew it, my one-week mini holiday at my sister's was over, and it was time to leave for Philadelphia—or Philly as it's popularly called—where my school was located. Now, I was truly on my own, with no family waiting for me on the other side.

I'd thought leaving Nigeria was hard, but I only realized the weight of what I had signed up for once school began. I was going to have to start building new memories, new friendships, new experiences, and new communities. During my first week settling in, my family and my boyfriend constantly called to check on me. I'm grateful for those moments in the day when my phone rang, and I was greeted by the loving, familiar faces of the people I cared about the most.

I spent the first few days on campus familiarizing myself with the program's demands, learning my way around the new environment, and completing my registration. I also attended the interview for the Graduate Assistant position at the Tutoring Center. That day felt particularly significant because it was my first time interviewing for a role in an international context. I prepared as best as I could by reviewing the job description, reflecting on how my past experiences connected to the role, and researching the Center online.

On the day of the interview, I set out carrying my handbag and wearing the clothes and shoes my mum had bought for me before I left Nigeria. I felt smart in my outfit then, but I laugh when I look at the pictures now. So much has changed about how I look and dress, but I believe what mattered most was that I felt confident.

During the interview, I was asked several questions I no longer remember in detail, but I remember speaking passionately about my love for education and the work I had done so far, especially as a teacher in the Teach For Nigeria fellowship. While I didn't yet have many of the analytical skills the role required, my undergraduate background in Economics gave me a strong foundation to learn on the job.

At the end of the interview, I was informed that they had other candidates to meet and that I would hear back within a week if I were successful. Waiting, as always, was nerve-wracking, but I felt confident that God, who had brought me this far, would provide for me one way or another. I really loved the job description, and I enjoyed the interview so much. I hoped that I would get the opportunity to work with the Center.

In just 24 hours, my prayer was answered. I got an email congratulating me on my successful application. Later, my supervisor told me that my passion and heart for students had been evident in the way I spoke, and in her heart, she just knew I was the right fit. She added that my easy-going attitude during the interview made her confident that it would be a delight working with me. And she wasn't wrong, *if I do say so myself.*

With the interview behind me and a job successfully secured, I was free to spend the remaining days of my arrival fully focused on orientation.

As with every new undertaking, there is always an orientation period. This could be a formally organized process or an informal one arranged by the school. Either way, orientation is a key part of every new beginning. For us, international students, this phase starts the moment we arrive at the airport. Everything feels new and unfamiliar. It's then that you realize that, alongside your academic journey, you've taken up a whole new challenge of adapting to an entirely new culture and system.

Chapter 8

Just Flatmates

If possible, as far as it depends on you, live at peace with everyone. (Romans 12:18, AMP).

Before traveling to the US, I'd already decided I was going to live on campus. I was entering a new country and navigating unfamiliar systems, so I didn't want the added stress of figuring out housing logistics.

I had heard stories of students being scammed by online agencies or arriving to find their off-campus apartments looked nothing like the photos. I didn't want to add that to my list of first-year challenges. So, campus accommodation felt like the safest option. It guaranteed proximity to classes, a decent standard of living, and, most importantly, peace of mind in those early days of adjustment.

Of course, if you're up for the adventure or trying to save significantly on costs, off-campus living might be a better fit. But for me, at that point, I just wanted something predictable and safe.

Thanks to the P.E.O. International Peace Scholarship I

had received, I was able to afford campus housing in my first year, which made the decision even easier. I planned to stay on campus for at least the first semester, get familiar with the area, hopefully make a few friends, and then consider moving off campus later.

Because of the way campus housing was set up, I didn't get to choose my flatmate. It was more like: *"Here are the rooms available, here are the rates, and here's the sign-up sheet. You can include any special preferences if you have them."* After that, I was automatically matched with someone.

In my first year of graduate school, I lived with a Chinese flatmate who was in her second year. It was my first time sharing a home with someone from a completely different culture—my first non-African housemate—and though I tried not to overthink it, I'll admit I felt a bit anxious.

Before coming to grad school, I'd heard stories of students dealing with awkward roommate dynamics— clashing over chores, differing living habits, and mismatched expectations in shared spaces. I knew these challenges weren't unique to studying abroad, but somehow, my new context made them feel different.

Thankfully, my story turned out differently. I was blessed with an amiable flatmate, and our living arrangement worked well for both of us. Our different courses meant that we had alternating schedules, which naturally reduced the chances of clashing over shared spaces.

At the start of our stay, we had a brief and honest conversation about our expectations as flatmates. This helped us set, recognize, and maintain healthy boundaries from the beginning. There were weeks I bought fewer groceries or delayed cooking, just to be mindful of our limited fridge and kitchen space. On some days, I chose to cook at a later time because I knew certain Nigerian meals have strong aromas that might be unfamiliar to someone from another culture, so I adjusted when needed. I also made it a point of duty to keep our shared spaces clean, even when I was in a hurry, because I didn't want little things like that to become sources of tension.

This habit of accommodating my flatmate was reciprocated on her end. She always cleaned up after using the kitchen, so I never had to worry about tidying before I could cook. The best part was that, since I loved meal prepping and she wasn't much of the cook-at-home type, she offered me the larger cupboard. She could have insisted on splitting the space equally—after all, we paid the same rent—but she didn't see the need for that, and she gladly gave me the extra space.

A big part of what I appreciated about my flatmate was the temperature control in the flat! Now, if you've just moved from Nigeria to study abroad, even the early fall weather, which starts around September, can feel cold because it's so humid back home. My flatmate, on the other hand, was used to the US climate and preferred it colder. Given that the thermostat control was in her room, she could have turned it up in the middle of the night or while I was out at class. Instead, she was considerate enough to keep it at a temperature that we could both tolerate, and we had no issues.

However, one day I returned from work to find the flat unusually cold. I was surprised, since I'd expected the heating to be on. I asked her about it, and she said she hadn't touched the control. Sensing the doubt in my voice, she even showed me the thermostat control in her room. I felt bad for doubting her, but I tried to justify it by asking why the flat was so cold. It turned out the problem was with the building's central heating, not the thermostat control.

That could have easily turned into a tense moment in the flat, but thankfully, she understood that I wasn't questioning her character. She reassured me that she had felt the same way when she got back from class, and had even checked the thermostat multiple times to make sure nothing had changed. Even when we had disagreements, which happened a few times, they were never chaotic. That, to me, is what a stress-free living arrangement looks like: two people acting with respect and maturity.

We never had a close relationship. It was more neutral—not exactly a friendship, but not frictional either, and that was enough. Sometimes, that's all you need, especially when your flatmate doesn't end up becoming a friend. But now, as I reflect on those days, I wonder if I could have tried harder. *What if I'd gone beyond simply coexisting and made more of an effort to connect?* Maybe, just maybe, I could have made a lifelong friend. But the stories I had heard, filled with tension and cultural misunderstandings, kept me cautious. I realize now that I was being conflict-avoidant. And while that worked for a while, eventually, I found myself feeling lonely in my own living space.

On the other hand, if you ever find yourself living with someone who isn't as understanding, just remember this: they won't be there forever. In the meantime, prioritize respect, clear communication, and a little patience. Through this initial living experience, I learned that even the most challenging living situations can teach you something, whether it's about setting boundaries, navigating differences, or simply learning what *not* to tolerate in the future.

Chapter 9

Things I'd Never Had to Question Before

But test everything that is said. Hold on to what is good.
(1 Thessalonians 5:21, NLT).

Before moving abroad, there were so many ideologies, beliefs, and convictions I had never paused to examine. These were assumptions I carried without question, simply because they had never been challenged. However, as the days and weeks unfolded, my capacity to understand and respect the customs, traditions, and lifestyles of others grew as well.

I was amazed at how little I knew about the rest of the world. The hardest part wasn't just learning new things; it was figuring out how to stay true to who I was while making space for new perspectives. I didn't want to come across as rigid or closed-minded, but I also didn't want to pretend I agreed with everything I heard.

I remember being in classrooms where topics like faith, religion, language, foreign aid, gender identity, and gender norms were being discussed. I often had to consciously compose my face to hide the shock I felt at hearing ideas that were completely alien to me. These views weren't just alien —they often didn't align with my beliefs or the way I saw the world. Still, I didn't want to come across as rude or dismissive, especially knowing that what was new or uncomfortable to me was someone else's reality.

For context, I grew up in a religious and conservative environment—both at home and through my years at school —so certain conversations simply didn't happen. Questioning belief in God or religious practices was not entertained. Expressing contrary thoughts or questioning existing practices could easily be seen as being "backslidden" or lacking in faith. Similarly, gender norms were generally unchallenged; these topics were closely tied to religion and left little to no room for questions or debate.

Even discussing sexual orientation was going too far. The word "sex" was spoken in hushed tones, let alone the idea of being a different sexual orientation other than straight. When these topics were addressed, it was usually in a punitive or negative context.

Being the good and obedient child I was, I followed the rules, rather than questioned them. So you can imagine what it felt like being in classrooms where these off-limits topics were a part of my academic discourse. It was, without a doubt, a culture shock for me.

There were discussions around racism, something I hadn't experienced growing up. Yet here I was in the white man's land, needing to engage in these somewhat difficult conversations. At first, I entered the classroom feeling a kind of solidarity with the other Black Americans. But over time, it became clear that shared skin colour didn't automatically mean shared experience.

I remember one day during a community outreach event, an elderly lady asked me, *"Where are you from?"* I answered *"Nigeria,"* and she responded, *'You do not know how lucky you are to be able to identify your roots and know exactly where you're from.'* At the time, I smiled politely, but I never forgot her words. It was the first time I realized that what I had always taken for granted—knowing my lineage, my tribe, my hometown—for some, was a painful gap. As I listened to the stories of Black Americans and dug deeper into the history and ongoing realities of racism, I became aware of a profound difference between us. Our skin color might be similar, but our histories, struggles, and cultural upbringings were not the same.

Surprisingly, I found myself connecting with some of my Indian classmates because we had similar experiences around upbringing and social norms. We had grown up in environments where gender roles were rarely questioned, rote learning was emphasised over critical thinking, and strict parenting with high moral and academic standards was the norm. It wasn't that these values were exclusive to us, but the way we talked about them, and the similar references we shared, made me feel seen. Of course, there were differences too, but in those moments, it felt like I'd found unexpected allies from a completely different continent.

Even with those moments of finding allies, I was constantly reminded that I was in a very different world. For example, I noticed places on campus that offered only vegan meals—not only for health reasons, but because people believed it was wrong to eat animal products. In Nigeria, I couldn't imagine life without a carnivorous diet; rice and chicken was our Sunday special back home!

Not everything was a culture shock, but some moments

still made me pause. One time, a professor questioned my choice of name. During one of our introductory classes, I introduced myself as "*Ody*," since the setting was quite warm and informal. This was out of habit because, back home, I was fondly called Ody. Odinaka, my full name, was usually reserved for formal contexts. After the class, she called me and said she was concerned I was shortening my name to make others comfortable. She said I didn't have to do that— everyone should learn how to pronounce it, and I shouldn't feel like I had to hide my identity.

While I understood her perspective and appreciated her care, the experience made me realize that I had entered an environment where almost every action was interpreted through the lens of someone's experiences or assumptions. Back home, being called "*Ody*" by family and friends was simply affectionate, but here, some read it as me down-playing my identity, or conforming to an easier way of name pronunciation for the Americans. It was all so fascinating!

At first, it all felt like walking on eggshells because I didn't want to come across as disrespectful or ignorant, even when my intentions were innocent. In those early days, I learned to listen more than I spoke. And in smaller groups, I asked thoughtful questions with the aim of understanding better.

Still, there were times it felt overwhelming. My views were constantly being challenged, and I began to recognize flaws in some of the ideas I had grown up with. In some cases, with wide eyes, I thought, *"Ody, there's more to this world than you realize. Your worldview is not the only one. Wake up!"* It wasn't the orientation I had imagined, but I had to grow—and fast.

Engaging in these conversations required openness.

Being open didn't mean adopting someone else's viewpoint as my own. It meant truly listening, being willing to see the world through another person's lens, and engaging in meaningful, respectful dialogue, even around different world views. It also meant being open to having my beliefs challenged. The good thing about having these conversations in an academic setting was that there were clear ground rules for respect and constructive feedback. It wasn't a forced indoctrination of other people's beliefs.

As difficult and unsettling as these conversations were, I am grateful for them. They pushed me to build a solid foundation for the beliefs I claimed to hold. Back in Nigeria, it would have been easy to shy away from such discussions, but in this environment, I learned to confront my convictions with questions, dig deeper into my beliefs, and strengthen my faith. Make no mistake, all of these didn't happen in one class discussion or even in a single semester. It was a gradual re-orientation that unfolded over the years, shaped by studying abroad and interacting with people from diverse backgrounds.

Let's Talk about Faith

Allow me to sit on this topic of the Christian faith.

People often say that faith is blind, and in some ways, that's true. It asks us to trust in the unseen. But that doesn't mean faith is shallow. For me, studying abroad challenged me to unpack my beliefs. It pushed me to move from *borrowed certainty* to *personal conviction*. I had to truly understand what I believed, and why.

Studying abroad challenged my convictions. It pushed me to move from borrowed certainty to personal conviction.

I know some people fear engaging in these kinds of conversations or allowing unanswered questions to surface. Questions like, *"What if, in doing this, I lose my faith? What if I no longer believe?"* are common, and I understand the feeling. But then, as someone rightly told me, *"If you are scared to have your beliefs challenged, perhaps the faith was never there."*

God's Word is true, tried, and trustworthy. We don't need to be afraid of examining it closely—it won't fall apart under scrutiny. In fact, our willingness to ask questions and engage in honest conversations is often what helps us build a deeper, more unshakable faith, one that can stand firm through adversity and the shifting worldviews around us. It also becomes a powerful way to sift out the misguided ideas we may have absorbed along the way, including cultural beliefs that are not rooted in Scripture.

There is an intersection of religion and culture that deeply influences our beliefs. Much of what we hold as "truth" is often filtered through the lens of our upbringing. In many African contexts, for example, God is often portrayed as a stern Father—quick to discipline, ever watchful, and ready to punish us when we go astray. In contrast, in much of the Western world, God is more often seen as an ever-loving and understanding Father who is so gracious that He seems to overlook even habitual sin. While neither extreme captures the fullness of who God is, these cultural lenses shape how we relate to Him, and inevitably spill over into how we practice our faith and live out our devotion.

Because we often see God as a stern Father with a strict list of rules that must be obeyed to the letter, we tend to struggle when we enter environments where questioning, understanding, and critical thinking are encouraged. It becomes difficult to freely receive God's love when we've been shaped by a system that seems to demand perfection before acceptance.

From experience, I've found that taking time to examine one's faith and beliefs can help to reorient, redefine, and re-establish what it really means to walk with God—beyond the lens of culture or popular trends.

Some of us are in our bedrooms praying for a "global mandate," but God is looking at us and asking:

Are you ready to open your mind to what My perspective really looks like?

Are you ready to learn things beyond what you've always known?

Are you ready to step out of the box you have placed your-self in, so that My power can be made known and mighty through you?

Are you ready to stop clinging to stereotypes and embrace the unique prototype I created for you to be?

All of this comes with global exposure and a reawakened mindset.

There were other mindset shifts I began to notice, too. I realized I could confidently take up roles in the international development space. When opportunities came, I was ready for them. I could engage in meaningful conversations with people whose views differed from mine and still articulate my standpoint clearly, respectfully, and without shrinking.

There's something I must highlight in all of this talk about adaptation and expanding one's worldview: it is impor-tant to **stay true to who you are**. You can learn, adapt, and evolve, but you must remain grounded in your identity.

There might be the temptation to conform so as not to offend anyone, but it is possible to show up authentically without compromise. For example, many of my friends knew that on most Thursday or Friday evenings, I would likely be in the chapel—praying or studying my Bible. These friends were not Christians, yet I never felt the need to hide my devotion from them simply because we had different beliefs. That, to me, is what mutual respect looks like.

You can learn, adapt, and evolve, but still stay true to who you are.

I had a classmate who once told me that a night out partying with friends and a good bottle of wine were her go-to ways to de-stress. That wasn't something I personally related to, but it never stopped me from valuing who she was. She was brilliant and dependable, one of the first people I'd turn to whenever I needed help reviewing a scholarship application or editing an academic essay, and she always came through.

This might sound contrary to the things you have been taught or the idea that you should only keep the perfectly "righteous" circle of friends. Don't get me wrong, I still believe it's important to have close relationships that align with your values. But what I've come to learn is that it is also possible to engage meaningfully with people who don't see the world the same way you do, and to do so without diluting who you are.

I didn't compromise my beliefs, but I did expand my understanding. It dawned on me that the world was much bigger than the small circle I had once imagined it to be.

All in all, I would say my welcome into grad school was a bit of a smooth landing, even though it was a rollercoaster of emotions—navigating new experiences, diverse ideologies, and a whirlwind of activities.

But settling into a new cultural landscape was just one

part of the challenge. Beyond the external shifts, there was an even trickier battle unfolding— one within me. It's one thing to adjust to new customs and perspectives, but it's another to wrestle with the voice within that questions whether you truly belong.

And that's when an old, unwelcome visitor crept in.

Chapter 10

The Stranger That Comes Knocking

We now have this light shining in our hearts, but we ourselves are like fragile clay jars containing this great treasure. This makes it clear that our great power is from God, not from ourselves (2 Corinthians 4:7, NLT).

I was in a foreign land, so I expected many of my interactions to be with people of different races and ethnicities—practical strangers. However, there was one stranger that I did not expect to meet. This stranger appeared uninvited, was quite intrusive, and sowed self-doubt in me.

If you're still wondering who, or what, I'm talking about, it's Imposter Syndrome!

Imposter Syndrome is more than just a feeling of unpreparedness or anxiety. It's an enduring belief that you are fundamentally unworthy of your place, whether in an academic environment or elsewhere. It creates a disconnect between external validation and internal belief; a constant fear of being "found out" as a fraud. For me, graduate school was where I first fully confronted these feelings.

Graduate school, with its hyper-competitive atmosphere, high expectations, and relentless pressure to perform, was the perfect breeding ground for Imposter Syndrome. And let me tell you, it hit me in ways I never expected.

"What if it's not good enough?" was the question on repeat in my head.

No matter how hard I worked or how prepared I felt, there was always this underlying sense of doubt. I could spend hours perfecting a paper or rehearsing a presentation, yet right before submission or delivery, the familiar thought would creep in: *"What if it's not good enough?"* Every class discussion or research proposal began to feel like a test of whether I truly belonged, and it didn't matter how much effort I'd put in.

There were days I feared someone would look at my work and think, *"Really? That's it?"*

I remember one particular class I had signed up for; the professor was not only the Director of the Program but also the Chair of the Penn UNESCO fellowship, the full-tuition scholarship I was awarded. I'd never felt the need to prove myself as much as I did in his class! I wanted to appear intelligent and prove to him that I deserved the scholarship. It was already tough, feeling like I was falling behind in some other classes, so I vowed to prove that I was worthy of being fully funded by an Ivy League school.

The pressure was on.

Every night before class, I made sure I had thoroughly revised and felt as prepared as possible. Yet I always felt wound up. In class, anxiety hovered over me as I tried to be smart and well-read every time I contributed. It didn't help that, for some reason, the professor seemed to enjoy calling on me to answer tough questions or my perspectives on development issues.

He would go, *"Ody! What do you think about...?"* There were a few times I didn't have the answers or anything meaningful to add, and I felt a sharp pang of disappointment in myself.

Additionally, I had this paralyzing fear of making mistakes. I guess it stemmed from my perfectionist tendencies and the constant dread of being perceived as *"not good enough."*

The most challenging aspect of Imposter Syndrome, however, was the comparison trap. Graduate school has a way of putting everyone's brilliance on display. During my first seminar lecture, it felt like everyone, except me, knew exactly what was being discussed. My classmates asked such intelligent questions that I began doubting my own academic abilities. I knew I was intelligent, smart, and well-read, but when I got into my classes, I questioned the depth of my knowledge. I wondered if they had somehow studied all the course materials before resumption. *How did they know so much?*

I consoled myself with the fact that we all came from different educational backgrounds and had varying levels of exposure over time.

Yet even with that reassurance, I still felt like I was behind.

Every class, conference, and published paper felt like a spotlight on someone else's success. I couldn't help but compare myself to everyone around me. And it wasn't just about academics—I compared everything, from how quickly people grasped concepts to how confidently they expressed their ideas. With each comparison, my sense of inadequacy only deepened.

Imposter Syndrome made me question whether I truly deserved my place in grad school. In the midst of these feelings of unworthiness, I thought I was alone. In retrospect, I realize that I wasn't the only one struggling with these feelings. Many of us experience these doubts at some point, but we just don't talk about them.

I think COVID-19 was also a game-changer. The uncertainty it brought forced us to realize that everyone was, in some way, *winging it*, and nobody had all the answers. For the first time in a long while, our limitations were accepted as a part of our humanity, rather than as weaknesses.

In school, there was a newfound empathy between staff and students, and among colleagues. The academic world suddenly felt less cut-throat because, at that moment, it was no longer about competition; it was about survival. Grades seemed almost irrelevant. *I mean, the world was ending, who grades epp?*[1]

But before that moment, it felt like I was alone, trapped in a cycle of self-doubt, overwork, and constant comparison. I was doing everything I could to keep up, while secretly feeling like I was always falling behind. I found myself reading more articles than I probably needed to, reworking papers for hours, and obsessing over the smallest details. It wasn't just about doing well; it was about proving, to myself and everyone else, that I deserved the scholarship.

I thought that if I worked hard enough, I could silence

---

1. *Who grades epp?* is a common Nigerian colloquial expression that roughly translates to, *"What's the relevance of grades in a situation like this?"*

the voice telling me I wasn't good enough. But no matter how many late nights I spent in the library or how many drafts I wrote, the feeling never went away. So, I kept telling myself that I just needed to work harder.

What I didn't realize was that by taking on the mission to "prove myself," I was also implying that I didn't believe in who I already was. I doubted my intelligence, my abilities, and even my worthiness of the scholarship, so I sought out external validation to confirm it. Ironically, this mindset took the joy out of learning. Every class became a test to prove something I already was. In reality, all I needed to do was believe that, even though I was in a different environment, I was still the same Odinaka who was capable of great things.

The wake-up moment for me came during the early weeks of my second term, specifically on Valentine's Day. I woke up that morning feeling unbearably heavy, and then I broke down crying. It wasn't the quiet kind of sobs. It was loud and ugly. I was emotionally overwhelmed. I had thought school would be fun, but everything felt like an uphill climb. I was tired, exhausted, and deeply frustrated.

This was supposed to be a program I loved, but your girl was tired! I sent an email to my lecturer communicating that I couldn't make it to class that day because I felt unwell. I wasn't sure I could survive even one more day of school.

While I was sitting in that fog of exhaustion and over-whelm, I heard a knock on my bedroom door. At first, I considered ignoring it, hoping the person would eventually walk away. But something in me decided to open it.

It was my classmate Elisa, who lived in the same building. She stepped in with the brightest smile, and I remember wondering what could possibly be so cheerful about that morning. She said she had a gift for me.

Now, Elisa had a way of popping in with little thoughtful gifts, so at first, I assumed her visit that morning was no different. But I wasn't in the mood for anything. I just wanted to be by myself. She handed me a package and said it was a gift from a friend. I couldn't think of which friend would have sent me a package on Valentine's Day, and I certainly wasn't thinking of my boyfriend, now husband, who was in Nigeria.

I opened the package, and to my absolute surprise, it was from him! My shock at seeing the gift quickly gave way to overwhelming emotion as I saw what it was. It was a personalized affirmation frame. As I read the words, I wept even louder.

I called him and couldn't stop crying because I desperately needed to hear those words. The pressure I had been placing on myself had taken a toll on my mental health. When he picked up, he said to me, *"Ody, those are your words."* I was stunned. I would have remembered writing them. He explained, *"When you got admission, you wrote those words in your journal, and you sent them to me on WhatsApp. You asked that I always help you remember them. All I did was personalize it and send it back to you in a frame."*

It was such a timely gift; I had never realized how powerful affirmations are. But this wasn't just a random affirmation; it was a reminder of God's Word over my life, speaking truth and encouragement when I needed it most.

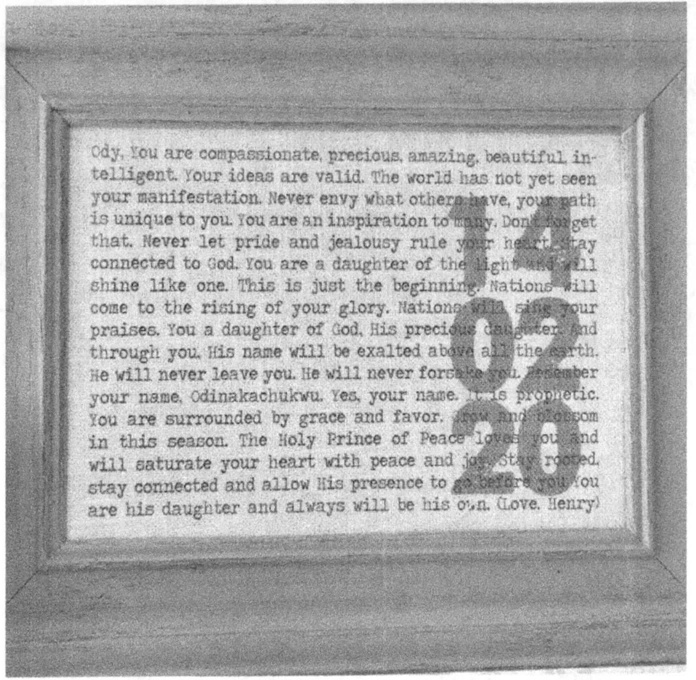

The affirmation frame from my boyfriend (now husband). It was a powerful reminder that came in at the right time.

From that moment, I found the strength I needed to navigate the rest of my academic journey. And every time doubt tried to creep in, I would glance at my frame by my bedside and be reminded of who I was.

Of course, there were still moments that tested my rediscovered identity. But slowly, I began to enjoy school again, and learning became a fun-filled activity. I no longer felt the need to prove who I already was. I became open to taking on new challenges, and even failing, as long as it gave me the chance to learn and grow.

I remember that the following semester, I faced one of my biggest fears and took a class in Advanced Quantitative Evaluation. It was a class I never would have considered before, fearing my mathematical skills weren't strong enough. But there I was, trying new things and attempting hard ones too! No longer was I bound by the chains of Imposter Syndrome.

For the person reading this who just got into graduate school and feels like *"I'm struggling, and I need help,"* I can tell you this: life becomes truly fulfilling when you live with the knowledge of who you are and the confidence that comes with it. But I also know there will be days when that confidence wavers, and moments when you need a reminder.

So, here's something I encourage you to do: write down an affirmation that speaks to your identity, your strength, and your ability to navigate this season. Place it somewhere visible, so that on the tough days, when doubt creeps in, you have a truth to hold onto.

I was walking on cloud nine with this newfound freedom, and while there were many other tough and challenging moments, they didn't shake my self-esteem or sense of identity. That was, until one final moment in my last term. It was a moment that truly tested me, and I'll share more about it in the next chapter, which focuses on building academic resilience.

Just so we remember, let's call this "favorite" professor, Mr A.

Chapter 11

Akada, Tighten Your Seatbelt

But he said to me, "My grace is sufficient for you, for my power is made perfect in weakness." Therefore I will boast all the more gladly about my weaknesses, so that Christ's power may rest on me (2 Corinthians 12:9, NIV).

I failed my first assignment.

And I didn't just fail; the professor requested that I see her in her office. I had never been so scared in my life. A flood of thoughts raced through my mind.

Would they withdraw my scholarship?

Would they give me a second chance?

Would I fail the course?

How could I have made such a bad impression on my first task?

I was terrified.

I must have read that email at least five times. My heart sank deeper with each line. I felt like I had messed up in a big way. If you are wondering what my mistake was, it was the APA citations. I had submitted an assignment without properly referencing my sources, and that cost me dearly.

After reading the email one more time, I replied, letting the professor know I would see her during her office hours. That night, I poured my heart out in prayer. By the following day, she had replied, confirming I could come and see her.

I walked into her office, weighed down by shame. Being a perfectionist, this felt like a major blow. Perhaps she saw the remorse and restlessness written all over my face, or maybe God chose to show me mercy, but her voice was far kinder than I had imagined, even more so than the tone of the email.

I didn't waste time. I quickly apologized for my error and promised to do better next time, ensuring my work was properly referenced.

Thankfully, she gave me a second chance, since it was my first time being penalized for an error of that nature. I believe she also empathized with me—she could probably tell I was still adjusting to the academic system. Being allowed to redo the assignment, even with a reduced grade, felt like a gift. It was way better than any other penalty she could have imposed.

As soon as I left her office, I went straight to the Academic Counseling department to book sessions on APA referencing and academic writing. That verse in Nahum 1:9 that says, *"Affliction shall not arise a second time?"* kept running through my mind. I promised myself that a repeat situation would never happen. One mistake is human; a second time would be a choice, and that wouldn't be me.

I approached my next submission differently. I carefully studied the assignment brief, outlined my ideas with guidance from the Writing Center, and meticulously tracked every single source. I even returned to the Academic Counseling team to get feedback on my draft before submitting it. This experience became a turning point—it taught me the value of thoroughness in how I approached my assignments going forward.

From that experience, I became so thorough that even writing a social media post without proper referencing felt wrong. I realized how different the academic standards were from back home. For this reason, I always advise anyone entering graduate school, especially if you're from a background where academic writing wasn't emphasized, to prioritize learning proper referencing styles and academic writing techniques as soon as you arrive on campus. Trust me, it will save you a great deal of stress.

Building Academic Resilience

Remember Mr A, my favorite lecturer from the previous chapter? My love for academics had never been tested like it was in his class. I think it was after that experience that any fleeting thoughts of pursuing a PhD right after my master's were completely banished. I would need a long while to recover from that one!

From the very first day I walked into the class, I was whispering prayers in my heart, hoping I would enjoy it. But everything about the course felt different from any other course I had taken before: the teaching style, the room setup, and even the structure of the module itself. For some reason, nothing about the course appealed to me.

Still, I tried hard not to dismiss it outright, especially since passing was non-negotiable—it was a mandatory requirement for graduation. On top of that, the skills gained from the course would look excellent on my professional resume. So, I reasoned that to pass with flying colours, I figured I had to at least like it.

What a situation.

At first, I wondered if I was the only one feeling lost, but soon I realized that a majority of my classmates were just as confused as I was. Since it was a core module, I knew I had to do well, no matter what. I took every step I could: attending office hours, having multiple discussions with classmates about the material, re-reading the texts, and dedicating extra time to assignments.

And yet, it still felt like the core concepts were slipping through my grasp. It was, without a doubt, the most frustrating period of my academic journey.

What helped me survive was a few friends who, thankfully, were also trying to decode the class. We'd meet up in the evenings, huddle in the library, and do our readings together. It didn't magically make the content any easier, but it made the whole experience so much more bearable. Those times in the library are now some of my fondest moments from grad school: those nights when the readings became so intense, and we'd pause to crack jokes to lighten the mood. Writing this now, I can't help but smile just thinking about our little study group and how we managed to laugh our way through the chaos.

Perhaps if this course had been optional, I would have dodged it. But since it was required for graduation, there was no escaping it. So, what did I do? I faced it head-on. I gave it my absolute best.

Now, wouldn't it be nice if this story ended with, *"And I got an A!"* Well, guess what? All my efforts didn't save me from this grade:

. . .

Odinaka,

The good news is that you have the components and the mechanics of the policy analytic approach here. So you have the structure. And you have a good start on the nature of the problem.

But as our comments indicate, you don't really have an analysis here. You don't compellingly define and defend the criteria, and then you pick a wide array of policy options that are too broad, and finally, you don't have much of a research base here. I'm sorry, but I'm being very frank here because there isn't really a way to sugarcoat this message.

Nigeria is a country that has had a lot written about it — DfID has done a ton through the Edoren and other programs, but you don't seem to have found much of this and other relevant research.

We need to talk about a way forward. One idea would be to consider doing a Discussion Paper as the final product and taking another shot at this. Another might be to revise this to improve the grade and then do the policy brief, but that will extend the time frame for finishing. Maybe not a bad idea.

Anyway, please be in touch with us to set up a time to talk with one of us soon.

Grade C+

I received disappointing feedback after all the effort I put into the assignment!

For the first time, I called my parents to cry about my grades. And when I spoke to them, I found myself using a phrase I often corrected my own students for saying, *"The teacher gave me this score."* Normally, I dislike that phrase because it absolves us of responsibility when we blame negative happenings on others.

But this time, I didn't care because I felt crushed.

This was an assignment that I believed I had poured my best into, even while struggling to fully grasp the material. Yet, my best wasn't good enough because *what was this C grade I was seeing alongside this feedback?* It was devastating. You might be thinking, *"Well, a C isn't that bad."* However, knowing the sweat and toil I'd put in, ah! It was very depressing.

When I received the assessment, I didn't know what to do. True to my usual approach since entering grad school, I cried first. I would usually cry first to let go of whatever tension and disappointment I felt. Then, after crying, I would speak to myself and say, *"Oya[1], you have cried, what next? Is it a case of prayer or action, or maybe seeking counsel outside?"* But this time, my tears were heavier. It was not just a cry of frustration, but of complete emotional exhaustion.

At first, I told myself to just move on. After all, a C was still a pass, and my other courses validated my intelligence. But a few days later, I picked up the paper again, re-read the feedback, and I was back to square one. I was so disappointed. Almost every comment felt like a sting. As my Nigerian people would say, *"Who did I offend?"*

It took another two weeks before I could face the paper again. When I did, I scheduled a call with the professor. I explained how the grade and feedback had left me confused and disheartened, especially considering the effort I had put

---

1. Nigerian pidgin English used to encourage action. It can roughly translate to, *"Let's go,"* or *"Hurry up."*

in. To my surprise, he listened; he *really* listened. That opened the door for me to speak freely and process everything out loud.

I don't know what happened during that call, but God was definitely at work. The professor acknowledged my concerns, gave me clearer direction on how to proceed, and even offered support if I chose to rework the paper.

After the call, I felt so much lighter. For a moment, I wondered, *"Why didn't he offer this support earlier?"* Then another thought popped up, *"Why did you open up so much about your disappointment and your vulnerability? You must seem like a weak student in his eyes. Don't ever ask him for a recommendation letter."* But honestly, all of those were just prideful, self-critical thoughts, and I'm glad I did not pay them any heed. Instead, I asked for help, and thank God I received the guidance I needed.

I started to work on the paper again with a clearer direction. I also sought help from my classmates who had done well in the module, had a better understanding, and were willing to guide me. The support I received was overwhelming, and I'm grateful for those classmates. The professor also gave me a new deadline, in consideration of the COVID-19 pandemic, because of COVID, there was more leniency with assignment submissions and grading deadlines. With the extra time and another round of sleepless nights, I finally turned in the revised paper three weeks later.

As I hit "submit", I felt nervous. *What if my efforts still didn't yield the results I hoped for?* By that point, I was done with fear and obsessively cross-checking the assignment for the umpteenth time (*okay, that's a little exaggeration*). I prayed, and let it go.

A few weeks later, I saw the email notification in my

inbox—the moment of truth. My heart raced, but nothing prepared me for what I saw: an A!

Dear Odinaka,

We appreciated how your nature of the problem section explores the multiple causes and challenges to improving education, while still narrowing in clearly on teacher content knowledge and pedagogy in a particular region. It seemed like the boundaries of a complex problem are well-articulated.

With objectives- remember, they can be closely tied to the problem statement (as yours is), but also touchstones, or aspirational- so perhaps something like "improving student learning outcomes' or larger goals could also be included as an objective (to provide motivation and frame this within a larger goal to your MoE audience).

Regarding your criteria, these are much improved. Your explanation, for instance, of the effectiveness measure is quite good, calling upon a wide range of researchers, both Nigerian and global. It would be good to have some idea why "high" is above 75%, etc, and if any other reasonable comparators have achieved this level.

Your policy options and analysis are clear, and you do a great job of calling upon the literature to both formulate and support them (especially Option 1). Your matrix and recommendations section, where you weigh trade-offs, was compelling; your use of evidence from previous interventions in Nigeria was also very compelling to me as a reader. We appreciated how you applied each criterion to each option very methodically, and it was easy to follow your analysis.

There are a few distracting typos with run-on sentences and missing punctuation; it would have benefited from a proofread. But overall, this is solid work and shows tremendous improvement.

Paper Grade: A-

Semester Grade for Participation and Effort: A-

After putting in the work, but with a better understanding of the course, I got an A!

I didn't just celebrate the grade, I celebrated the growth I saw in the feedback. Tears came—happy ones this time. *I hope you're not tired yet of my tears, hehe.* I read through the entire feedback and realized that this paper was truly my best work yet.

The difference between my initial and second submissions was striking. What I had thought was my "best" had grown into something better. That paper became one I proudly shared at interviews as a sample of my academic writing prowess.

I'm glad I went through the rigorous process.

I'm glad I got back up after the crushing disappointment.

I'm glad for friends and family who supported me through the trying moments of redoing the assignment.

I'm grateful I went through this because it built a different kind of resilience in me. I pushed myself in a way that I had never done, and it yielded results.

It taught me that I could do difficult things.

It taught me I could rise after a setback; that setbacks don't mean *stop*, and that there's strength in starting over.

Looking back now, I also see how even in those tearful nights and frustrating rewrites, God's grace was quietly holding me up. His strength showed up, not when I had it all together but when I admitted I didn't. The anchor scripture of this chapter became for me a reminder that grace isn't for the perfect; it's for the willing.

Grace isn't for the perfect; it's for the willing.

While I celebrated the resilience I built in the academic environment, graduate school had other lessons waiting—

lessons that wouldn't appear on a transcript, but would show up on my body, my confidence, and my sense of self.

Chapter 12

Keeping Fit Amidst the Burgers and Fries

So whether you eat or drink or whatever you do, do it all for the glory of God (1 Corinthians 10:31, NIV).

I woke up one morning to get ready for class, reached for my favorite jeans... and they didn't fit.

Wait. What?

I tried a different pair. Still tight. I pulled out one of my Ankara gowns that I had sewn from home, hoping it would save the day. Nope. It refused to zip up, too.

Ah, this is more serious than I thought.

I knew my clothes were starting to feel a little snug, but I'd been too busy admiring my backside and hips to realize what was really happening: I was gaining weight. At first, I told myself that my expanding curves were just a sign of good living—the kind of *grown-woman thick* that everyone loves. But alas, this was not *thick*. It was excess fat.

That day, after class, I bought a digital scale, stepped on it, and was shocked to see the numbers. *"This must be wrong."* I thought to myself, *"All these digital scales, some-*

times they like to misbehave. This cannot be my weight. Let me try again in the morning when I'm fresh out of bed. It must be that I drank too much water."

The next morning, I stepped on the scale again, and the numbers hadn't budged. The scale was not lying, so I had to tell myself the truth. *"Ody, you have gained weight o!"*

It was then that I started noticing my puffy cheeks and bloated belly. Now, don't get me wrong—I know the picture I'm painting may sound like I was round and ugly, but far from it. I still looked beautiful. And that was the deception in the first place, because I had mistaken excess fat for becoming thick in the right places. Well, I thank God I realized it sooner rather than later.

That evening, I came back from class exhausted, but I still had a couple of assignments to finish up. In my usual fashion, I brought out my favorite brioche bread from the fridge and settled in with a steaming cup of chocolate tea. This was usually my way of unwinding after a long, cold day outside.

I was on a call with my friend, lamenting about my weight gain, when she burst out laughing: *"And you're saying this while eating bread and drinking chocolate tea?"*

Defensively, I told her it was just bread and tea. After all, I used to eat the same thing almost every day back home, and I never gained a pound.

However, it was when she pointed it out that it hit me: the culprit wasn't take-outs or burgers and fries (I could count on one hand how many times I had burgers in the US). No, it was the small, subconscious decisions that had crept into my routine.

It was the nighttime cup of steaming chocolate tea and a brioche loaf.

It was the packs of M&M's I munched on to stay awake during long lectures.

It was the packs of chocolate candies and biscuits that I grabbed from stores on my way back from school.

It was the creamy caffe mocha I usually got at the start of my day from Starbucks.

It was the free snacks served at every college event.

All these tiny indulgences were adding up to my weight gain—and fast.

Back in Nigeria, I hovered between 57–59 kg, but here I was in the 65–67 kg range—almost a 10 kg difference, and in just three months! *What would happen at the end of my degree?!*

Immediately, I knew the first thing to do was to cut down on all the chocolates I had been heartily consuming. But oh, that was war! That was when I realized sugar was indeed an addiction. I had always joked about how much I loved M&M's, but I never imagined that giving them up would be a battle.

You wouldn't believe it if I told you I experienced withdrawal symptoms after I tried to cut it out—but I did. Headaches. Mood swings. Grumpiness. It turned out that I had been reaching for sugar anytime I felt bored, tired, or overwhelmed, without realizing how dependent I'd become on it.

That week was miserable. I had no chocolates to cheer me up; no M&M's to soothe my soul.

Then, on the last day of that week, a classmate stopped by my flat to say hello. She held out a few bags of chocolate and said, *"Oh, I was given these bags of chocolates as a gift, but it's a little too much for me. I know you love M&M's,*

though I haven't seen you eating any this week in class. Would you mind having these bags with me?"

My mind was screaming, *"No, thank you."* But my voice was mute. Eventually, I managed to tell her I was trying to stop taking chocolates, especially M&M's, and she laughed. *"Wow. Never thought I'd see the day Ody would say no to M&M's."*

As she was leaving, she said, *"You know, I have a half-finished bag of chocolates; perhaps we can share that one instead, so you don't have to consume this big size."* I thought to myself that half a bag would not be a bad idea. Having a little bag wouldn't hurt. And the rest of the story, my friend, is history.

Just like that, I was back where I started. Or perhaps worse, because my body was doubly excited to welcome the chocolates back. As a consolation, I told myself that my current consumption didn't matter since I could abstain from it again for another week.

Spoiler alert: that wasn't the case.

It was supposed to be a simple matter of discipline—just stop eating chocolate. Easy, right?

Wrong.

Eventually, I started thinking about it from a spiritual perspective. I didn't like how much control this one thing had over me; how a tiny pack of chocolate could call the shots. So, I did something I'd never tried before: I prayed about it. I asked God to help me say no. It felt so small at first, so *silly*. Imagine bothering God with chocolate prayers? To be honest, that was one of the first times I really understood that there is no area of our lives too small for God's help.

Even my best pep talks failed miserably in the face of

temptation. So, I decided to go on a fast. Not just from chocolate, but as a way to reset spiritually and mentally.

Going through the fast was tough, especially given my previously poor diet, but I made it through. The fast became a time to reflect on my choices, my cravings, and what I wanted for my body and health.

Coming out of it, I started searching online for support, maybe a coach or a structured plan. But everything I found was pricey. As a student, I couldn't afford those programs.

So, I decided to start with doing the things I knew were helpful for weight loss:

- I cut down on sweets and junk food.
- I cooked more at home.
- I took longer walks and enrolled in the free campus gym.
- I stopped eating bread and tea at night before I slept.
- I also reduced my caffe mocha intake and stopped asking for cream whenever I ordered.

These were small steps, but after two weeks, I started seeing changes. It made me happy, a thought, *"It's like this weight loss thing is not as hard as I thought it would be."*

But that was before I started at the gym.

My first time there was completely overwhelming. I had no idea where to start, and most of the machines looked like alien contraptions. What's more, everyone around me looked like they belonged on the cover of a fitness magazine. I went to the free weight area and saw people lifting 25kg dumbbells. Meanwhile, I was searching for a 2.5kg dumbbell, all the while trying to keep my belly sucked in. That first visit was intimidating.

After that, I decided to find an accountability buddy. Also, I gave myself endless pep talks to avoid comparing myself to others. I reminded myself, *"Don't worry, everyone started from somewhere before they got toned or could do such heavy lifting."* I also reminded myself that everyone was once a newbie at some point, figuring out the gym exercises and equipment.

By the second night, I ran into two male classmates at the gym. We weren't close, but they quickly became my gym buddies. Before long, the gym felt like my second home. I started seeing results, and I loved it. Within a month, I was on a solid streak, and it brought me so much joy.

To add to my joy, I stumbled upon a lady's fitness page on Instagram. She was offering a Christmas discount on her coaching program, which included meal plans, weekly work-outs, and accountability check-ins. Best of all, it was affordable.

I was so excited about my find, and I immediately signed up for the program. Her plan gave me structure and took the guesswork out of figuring out what to eat or how to train. I followed it diligently. I remember my friend visiting me on campus, and she kept saying, *"Ody, tell me the secret. Your body is looking so toned!"* At work, my colleagues also noticed, and they would indirectly ask questions about what my new routine was, for fear of sounding rude or insensitive.

However, there was this older lady who did not mind any of that etiquette—and not in a good way. She bluntly told me, *"You are getting too big. You are growing too much muscle. Whatever you are doing, you need to stop. It's not good for a lady to look manly."* I just smiled and replied, *"I actually love how my body looks now, and I'm not stopping."* That was the end of the conversation.

I had fallen in love with this version of me: disciplined, healthier, and finally in control. I wasn't going to be bothered by someone else's contrary thoughts or opinions.

As long as I looked good in the mirror, I was fine. *And boy did I look good!* Plus, with a consistent meal plan, I wasn't struggling with poor eating habits anymore. It helped that the plan wasn't boring either—it still included the foods I loved, but in the right portions, and with more vegetables and protein.

I was enjoying this new phase until it was Christmas break. I went to visit my sister, Nneka, and let's just say, she knows how to enjoy life—food included.

At first, I told myself, *"It's okay, you have made healthy choices over the past few months, one day...one week wouldn't hurt."* But soon, my carefully built habits were drowned in pizza slices, buttermilk pancakes, creamy seafood pasta, spaghetti bolognese, and garlic bread starters at restaurants.

It's crazy how appealing these foods are, and once you start, you just want more. I even tried to order a salad one time to redeem myself, but the poor thing looked so sad beside the juicy steak and fries that I just said, *"Bye salad, some other time."* Thankfully, that *"some other time"* wasn't too far away. I was shocked to realize how just two weeks of indulgence could start undoing two months of consistent progress. That's when it clicked that staying fit in America required a different kind of long-term discipline. Back home in Nigeria, my weight didn't bounce around like this. I could eat *eba*[1] and rice back to back, or just oats and *moimoi*[2], and still hover around the same number on the scale. But here in America, every food decision seemed to show up on my belly, cheeks, and hips.

I think a large part of the problem was the food itself. Back in Nigeria, 90% of what I ate was home-cooked. Here, cooking required serious intentionality, and even "healthy" grocery items could be misleading. I remember picking up a brand of yogurt only to discover that it had more sugar than ice cream. And don't get me started on cereal. Packaged foods were filled with additives and hidden sugars—ingredients that made gaining weight all too easy.

I encountered what I now call the "false healthy diet." I'd pick up items labeled "*100% pure apple juice, sugar-free, low-fat yogurt, reduced calorie, plant-based, etc.*" List them. But these labels were marketing gimmicks. Many "sugar-free" foods were packed with artificial sweeteners, and a simple salad at the restaurant could sabotage your fitfam[3] life with heavy calorie dressings, croutons, or cheese.

Navigating food in America was stressful. I missed the simplicity of walking to a local market in Nigeria and picking up fresh, familiar ingredients. Here, I had to be extra conscious, reading every label and checking every ingredient. To stay healthy, I had to re-educate myself about nutrition from scratch.

---

1. Nigerian staple food made from dried cassava flour and eaten with a variety of soups.

2. Moimoi is a bean pudding or steamed bean pudding; a popular Nigerian dish made with steamed or boiled beans, onions, peppers, and spices, often including fish, eggs, chicken, or crayfish.

3. Fitfam is a term used to describe people who are dedicated to fitness and a healthy lifestyle

Cooking at home had to become a regular habit. It was the best way I could control the ingredients used in my food, so batch cooking over the weekend became a thing.

I had my ups and downs with managing my weight in the US, but two things carried me through: consistency and discipline. One of my best fitness coaches used to say, *"Weight loss requires self-discipline, consistency, and patience, the process of which makes the results sustainable over time."* She was such a gift on my fitness journey. What I loved most was that she brought a biblical perspective into health and wellness, something I'd never encountered before.

With her guidance, I stopped looking at food as good or bad and started thinking in terms of relationships. *What was my relationship with food?*

She taught me what it meant to practice self-restraint even when tempting options were right in front of me. It's one thing to clear your freezer of the foods that don't serve you, but the real test comes at birthday parties, summer picnics, or Christmas dinners with family and friends. *Could I still make intentional choices with creamy pasta and layered cake staring at me from across the table?*

It wasn't just a physical battle. It was mental. It was spiritual. With her, we even had Monday fasts as part of our routine, not just to give the body a break from constant digestion, but to build spiritual stamina. It instilled in me the truth that discipline doesn't start with food; it starts with focus.

Over time, I also learned that some of my struggles weren't just about food choices; they had deeper roots like stress, hormones, and even side effects from medication.

But even then, the lesson remained: be intentional with your food, don't eat more than your body needs, stay active, and drink water!

Chapter 13

The Pain Called Time Difference

There is a time for everything... a time to embrace and a time to refrain from embracing (Ecclesiastes 3:1 & 5b, NIV).

This chapter is dedicated to anyone navigating long-distance relationships—romantic or otherwise. Even if you are not in a romantic relationship, chances are that you'll leave behind a loved one when you relocate. It could be a sibling, a best friend, a cousin, your nephews or nieces, a neighbor, or someone from church. Distance changes things, and not every relationship survives the shift. Some evolve, others deepen, and some fade.

When I relocated, I gave little thought to what managing relationships back home would look like. I was caught up in the excitement of relocating to the US for my master's. Or perhaps, I got so absorbed in the planning and preparation that I didn't pause to consider how my relationships were going to change. It wasn't until the final week, when I began my goodbyes, that reality hit: I wouldn't see my boyfriend, Henry, perhaps for the next year, and I wouldn't be with my family either. I was going to miss my niece's first birthday and my nephew starting primary school. It was in those moments that reality hit. I felt an ache in my chest.

In my first week in the US, I was still riding the high of the move, busy with settling in. During that time, I was constantly FaceTiming my family, friends, and Henry, showing off my new surroundings, my apartment, groceries, classes, and every little detail. It felt different, but there was joy in sharing the experience with those I loved.

But eventually, the calls dwindled. Graduate school picked up, and the novelty of a new environment had worn off. There was so much happening that I barely had time to breathe, let alone talk on the phone.

And that's when the fights began.

I started feeling like I no longer had quality time with my boyfriend. I began demanding more of his time, asking him to realign his life with my new schedule. In all fairness, he was doing all he could to be present, but it just didn't feel like it was enough. Maybe I had underestimated how different things would feel. Maybe I thought one-hour calls would still feel the same. But they didn't.

Then there was my mum, too, who wished I would call more often to show that I was okay. It wasn't that I didn't want to call. I badly wanted to connect with all of them, but somehow being in the middle of the graduate school rush had put me in a different headspace. I was trying to adjust to the new demands of my schedule, so I barely had the strength at the end of the day to engage in a conversation.

In addition, I had that nagging feeling that they would not understand some matters if I brought them up, since it was a different context from being at home in Nigeria. I withheld information, and my conversations began to change because of this reality of living in two separate worlds.

With my boyfriend, I kept making demands. I missed him. I missed us. But the time difference made everything harder. I felt the vacuum deeply.

I remember one particular day, after finishing class early, rushing home to call Henry before he went to bed. At the time, Nigeria was six hours ahead, and we had been missing each other's calls all day. I couldn't wait to get home and tell him all about my day.

Immediately I got home, I called him. But just a few minutes into our call, he said, *"Babe, I have to go now, my battery is almost dead."* I couldn't believe my ears. I lashed out in frustration, asking why he hadn't charged his phone. *Didn't he know how badly I wanted to talk to him?* He explained that he had plugged his phone briefly when there was power, but later realized the switch was not turned on, so it didn't charge.

I don't know if anguish is the right word, but I was overwhelmingly sad. What he was saying to me at that moment was that we could not talk that night. It broke me because it was one of the nights when I felt like I really needed to talk to him. I needed my best friend to hear me out; I wanted to tell him about my day, I wanted him to listen to my struggles, encourage me, and remind me with those familiar words, *"You have got this, babe."* But here he was telling me he had to go. And it was not even his fault.

As soon as the call ended, I crumpled to the floor and cried. It felt like the weight of everything I'd been holding in came pouring out. The reality of long distance hit me hard.

There were other moments when he had to go to bed early because there was no electricity, or because he had an early appointment the following day. Sometimes, he just wasn't feeling well.

What I didn't realize was that the entire situation was just as hard for him as it was for me. I was so caught up in my own pain that I failed to notice his. After all, I was the one in a new country. I was the one going through culture shock, academic pressure, and loneliness.

There was one night he forgot his power bank in a public place he'd gone to charge, and I got really frustrated. Now that I write about it, electricity was our biggest enemy, not even the time difference or distance. Because even when we had some flexible time, there was the constant pressure to conserve his battery life. Henry, at the time, was working in a community with limited electricity and constant power outages, so charging his phone was always a struggle.

It was later that I learned how he sometimes had to go to public places to charge his phone; how he would save his power bank's charge just because he knew we had to talk; how he was spending so much on data than was normal, often switching between multiple SIM cards just to get a better internet connection. Some nights, he'd sleep only a few hours after staying up late with me and still have to wake up very early the next morning to prepare for his students. Despite all he was going through, he shielded me from the burden of his struggles because he knew how much I had on my plate.

It is only in hindsight that I see all the sacrifices he made. Back then, I was just hurting. All I knew was how much our relationship had changed—and not in the way I liked. It was difficult for me to be empathetic in that moment because I was so lonely, and I had shifted my emotional burdens to my best friend, who was the only safe space I knew.

The long distance was brutal on our relationship, but we tried. We started to find more ways to be creative about staying in touch despite the numerous challenges of time, electricity, internet, and availability. He got involved in my assignments and study time, and sometimes we would discuss my materials together, so those hours were still productive towards my studies. He also made every effort to call first thing in the morning (my time), which was around his own break time at school (he worked as a teacher in a school then).

Before I slept, I would leave messages for him that he was usually happy to wake up to. And then on the weekends, we had to try to maximize the time we had together, as the electricity back home permitted us. It wasn't the most ideal situation, but we had to make do with what we had. In between, when things didn't go as planned, there were still tensions. However, we kept pushing.

The real turning point came during Christmas break. After one intense semester, I traveled to see my sister, Nneka, with whom I'd stayed when I first arrived in the US. [By the way, it was also during this time that all my fit-fam results flew out of the window.] I was more than excited and looking forward to it because I was finally going to be with my family again.

While I was at her house, I realized something amazing: I was less dependent on Henry and made fewer demands on him! Because I was surrounded by activities, love, and family, I barely had time to feel lonely or sad. The tension we had experienced earlier in the semester started to make sense. It was that I had been leaning too heavily on Henry to fill a gap that could have been partially filled by my own community. As I was yet to build a solid community around me in school and hadn't joined activities that gave me joy, Henry ended up carrying the emotional weight of my social deficit.

Henry had encouraged me to expand my social circle and involve myself in more activities, but I had been too overwhelmed with adjusting to school and juggling my graduate job to even think about it. Plus, I was unsure where to start from, given that I was the only Nigerian and African in my class. I'd tried to connect with people from other backgrounds, but it wasn't the same. The Nigerian community hits differently with our food, the inside jokes, music, cultural days, and even Sunday worship.

That Christmas break opened my eyes. It revealed what I had been missing and what I needed to do to reduce the pressure in our relationship. I think Henry must have been the happiest when I came to that realization. After those weeks spent with my sister, I was ready and fully recharged to get back to campus. I'm truly grateful for that moment of respite. I can't imagine what the holidays would have been like if I had spent them alone. Who knows? Maybe I would have found another family to celebrate with—but in that moment, I was just grateful for my sister.

I went back to campus armed with the decision to engage more in school activities outside of my linear life of work, class, library, and cafe. I also learned to let go of the undue pressure and expectations I had put on Henry to be everything to me during that season. I think part of my fear was that if I found joy elsewhere, through people or activities, I would start drifting away from him. I feared that if we didn't get a lot of quality time, our bond would slowly fade. It was a real fear, and I struggled to get past it.

Somehow, we found a balance that worked. There were still moments when things got very intense at school, and I slipped back into old habits of putting all my burdens on Henry. I had made other friends, but no one really got me like Henry did—or so I thought.

There was a period when I went through an emotionally and physically draining time in school. I was so exhausted that I shut down and decided I could not handle a relationship anymore. I thank God for my close friends who called me to order and reminded me that what I was feeling and going through was just temporary. They said, *"It would be unwise to make a permanent decision based on a temporary situation."*

They were right. I needed space to recover mentally and emotionally, but I also knew I didn't want to add a heartbreak to the long list of things I was trying to manage in grad school, especially since there was no need for it.

Graduate school was truly demanding. Looking back, I often wonder what made it so difficult. I think the biggest challenge wasn't the academics, it was the absence of community. I'll speak more about this in the concluding chapters of this book.

I'm married to Henry, but that wouldn't have been possible if he hadn't looked beyond my shenanigans to the woman he had chosen to love before I left Nigeria. He held on because he believed the difficult season was temporary; that's why he chose to love and stand by me through it all.

Henry opened up to me that there was a point when he didn't think he could handle our relationship anymore because the weight of my emotional demands had become too much for him. In a weird twist of fate, that was also when COVID hit, and unexpectedly, it became a turning point because life slowed down and I had a chance to breathe, reflect, and take responsibility for my actions.

We had a hard conversation, and I wasn't proud of how I'd behaved in some moments. But I learned to show myself kindness and learn from it. That phase made our relationship even stronger. I knew in my heart that if we could survive my grad school phase, we could weather any storm together. That period strengthened our bond and taught me lessons about relationships in general:

1. Not every season will look the same. But how we keep showing up for the people we love is what matters the most. Relationships are not always 50-50; sometimes it will be 75-25, yet we have to keep showing up for the ones we love.

2. Remembering why you love someone and chose them in the first place will keep you going when things seem difficult.

3. You cannot expect one person to be everything to you, no matter how much that person loves you. Even best friends can feel burdened. Expand your circle, diversify your activities, and most importantly, lean on God. He's the One person who has promised to, and will, be there for you 24/7.

4. Never make a permanent decision about a relationship based on a temporary phase. Life will always stretch you in different ways. What holds relationships together is learning to show each other grace, kindness, and compassion during those testing times.

5. Sometimes, it might not end with a *"happily ever after."* Some friendships won't survive the changes life brings, and as painful as that can be, we have to let them go. This isn't failure; it's recognizing the evolving nature of relationships and appreciating the value that person brought to your life while they were there. It is difficult, I must confess, but shifting your perspective can help you grieve with grace and find peace in the lessons and memories they left behind.

I must add that managing expectations is quite crucial. It's imperative to recognize that the dynamics of some friendships will change. Some people won't be able to show up for you in the same way once you're no longer sharing the same physical space. And that's okay. They, too, are navigating their own life changes, just as you are.

Managing how you expect people to show up for you is important. But more than anything, extend grace too. When someone doesn't show up for you in the same way they once did, it doesn't mean they love you any less; they may just have less capacity in that season.

What matters is recognizing where they are and adjusting your expectations with kindness.

Chapter 14

The Most Asked Question, "So, What Next?"

Yet God has made everything beautiful for its own time. He has planted eternity in the human heart, but even so, people cannot see the whole scope of God's work from beginning to end (Ecclesiastes 3:11, NLT).

I'm not sure I will ever be able to fully express the helplessness wrapped up in the question *"What next?"*

Uncles, aunts, parents, friends, professors, and even distant relatives, wanted to know, *"What next?"* But for many of us, especially international students, this seemingly simple question carries an undercurrent of anxiety that's hard to shake.

I understand that most times, the question comes from a place of care. However, what most people do not know is that, sometimes, *"What next?"* feels less like concern and more like pressure.

It's especially intense in a one-year master's program. You spend the first few months just trying to stay afloat, learning the system, adjusting to culture shock, managing new academic demands, and maybe even working part-time. And just when you feel like you're getting the hang of it, *boom*! Graduation is already around the corner.

People say it is best to have a plan before grad school, and I agree—to an extent. But even the most carefully crafted plans aren't foolproof. You arrive with all your timelines, goals, strategies and then... life humbles you. The system surprises you. The world changes.

I was in my final semester when it hit me how quickly the year had flown by. I couldn't believe it was almost over. But that's what happens when you get caught up in the busyness of survival. Add a global pandemic to that recipe, and suddenly, everything you thought would happen doesn't.

I'd had plans to go to the UNESCO HQ in Paris for my program internship. I was really excited. It was an opportunity I had been anticipating since being awarded the Penn-UNESCO Scholarship. I had completed all the required preparations and was just waiting for my assignment when COVID hit. France was among the first countries in Europe to lock down, and just like that, the opportunity disappeared. This was the point at which I saw that my well-crafted plans were slowly dissipating into thin air.

Not having an international internship meant I missed out on the work experience I had hoped to showcase to potential employers. On top of that, networking events were cancelled, job markets were shrinking, and companies were laying off instead of hiring. Governments were uncertain. Even scientists didn't have answers.

2020 was the year nobody could predict. For a moment, it felt like the whole world was asking, *"What next?"* and no one had a clue.

The uncertainty of 2020 made employment prospects

feel even gloomier. To add to the tension, immigration policies were shifting constantly. I remember when the Trump administration, at the time, issued a directive requiring international students to leave the country if their classes were online. I was caught in a whirlwind of fear and confusion.

Ordinarily, many international students pursue the Optional Practical Training (OPT) route after graduate school in the US. This work authorization allows you to stay in the country and gain professional experience for one year — or up to three years if your program qualifies as STEM. At the time, the application fee was substantial, close to $500, and you had to secure employment within 60 days of the visa start date.

Applying for the visa was one thing; finding a job within the time frame was an entirely different challenge. I went ahead and submitted my OPT application while actively job-hunting. To my surprise, the visa was approved in just two weeks, meaning my 60-day countdown began immediately. I had heard stories of others whose visa approval took months, but mine was approved in barely a fortnight.

What should have felt like a blessing only intensified my worry: *"What if I don't get a job in time?"* I threw myself into applications, but opportunities were scarce. The economic downturn, combined with mass layoffs, had created an oversaturated job market, making each application feel like a long shot.

The first two weeks slipped by, and I hadn't gotten any leads. I kept hoping, praying, and trusting God as the clock ticked unceasingly. Then, out of the blue, a classmate reached out. She had spotted an opportunity on LinkedIn in an organization where she previously worked. I was grateful that she thought of me, but my excitement quickly faded when I saw it was a four-month internship. Initially, I hesitated to apply, but given the time constraints of my OPT visa, I realised I couldn't afford to be picky.

It helped that my friend spoke highly of the team and even offered to help me prepare. I was incredibly grateful for her support and poured my energy into the application. Less than a week later, I was invited to an interview.

Excitement coursed through me, but nerves weren't far behind. The organization was a well-known name in international education, and the role was mostly analytical, an area I didn't consider my strongest. But I had some experience from grad school and decided to give it my best shot.

The interview came, and I wasn't so sure I did well. Doubts crept in, and I began thinking ahead to what my next steps might be if I didn't get the role. Then came the email, every job seeker's favorite words: *"Congratulations, we are pleased to let you know that you have been offered the job."*

I couldn't believe my eyes. Happiness, relief, and gratitude washed over me all at once. The anxiety of a 60-day countdown could take a well-deserved break.

Later, I asked my manager why I had been selected, and she said it was because of my enthusiasm, passion, and the strength of my qualitative research experience. She believed I could grow into the analytical aspects of the role and was willing to take a chance on me. She not only gave me a chance at a job, but she also gave me an opportunity to build stronger analytical skills, contribute to a reputable organization, and to connect with colleagues who would challenge and support me.

For the next four months, I had structure. I hoped the internship might evolve into a full-time role, or at least buy me time to find another opportunity. Either way, I was grateful to be learning, contributing, and gaining valuable experience.

Those four months flew by faster than I could imagine, and before I knew it, I was in my last month. In that final month, one of the managers I had worked closely with was moving on to another organization. Her departure created an opening that matched my skill set perfectly, and I was excited at the possibility that lay before me. I also thought it was an additional bonus that I had been in the organization for the past quarter, because I had come to learn the systems and the culture while building rapport with the team.

With hope, I approached the recruitment team to express interest in the role. Then came the crushing blow: as an international student, I couldn't be considered because the organization couldn't sponsor visas. It was shocking to hear that because I had presumed an organization of that caliber would have the capacity to sponsor international employees. You can imagine how disheartened I felt.

I had worked hard, built relationships, and proven myself over those past months, but I still wasn't eligible. It was then that I began to fully understand the weight of being an international student. You could be qualified for a job and still not get it because of a lack of visa sponsorship.

From there on, more rejections came, most of them without even granting an interview. Most filtered me out the moment they saw I needed sponsorship. But I had to keep trying; there was no other option. Once my internship ended, I'd need another job to remain in the US.

I began reaching out to others who had navigated this phase. Many advised me to stop relying on cold applications and instead lean into personal connections. They told me plainly that the system wasn't designed to give international students a fair shot based on the need for visa sponsorship as a non-immigrant.

It was on one of those days, while reaching out to personal connections, that I came across a woman on LinkedIn. Her profile immediately caught my attention because her career journey mirrored so many of my aspirations, and the kind of work she had done deeply resonated with me.

I reached out to her for a chat, and to my joy, she responded. She was so kind and willing to make time to talk with me about her career journey. A few days before our scheduled call, I discovered that one of the organizations she had worked with was recruiting. I got excited because it would also be an opportunity for me to learn more about the organization. Their work in international development aligned so closely with my own interests.

The call was more helpful than I could have imagined. She shared honestly, offered thoughtful insights, and even went a step further to offer to recommend me for the open position in that organization. That alone boosted my confidence.

Around the same time, another classmate reached out to check on me and ask how my job search was going. When I mentioned that I was applying to the same organization, it turned out that she had also previously worked with the team's manager and was more than willing to recommend me to the hiring manager. I felt so blessed to have such support in my corner. After the interview, in less than a week, I was given the offer!

However, this was another 4-month internship. I accepted it with the mindset that I was going to utilize the opportunity to expand my network, grow my skills, and land something more permanent. Truth be told, it was an exciting internship. I was blessed with the most amazing manager and team.

It was during this time that I wrote my first internally published opinion piece, a milestone I'll never forget. I also met more people who were passionate about education and international development in that space.

I must pause here to mention my elder sister, Nneka. I had the privilege of staying with her during both internships. That safety net of having a roof over my head and not worrying about my next meal is something I am eternally grateful for. Her support gave me the peace of mind to keep going through an otherwise stressful season.

Oh, did I mention that the internship was also unpaid? If I'd been navigating all of this alone, I honestly don't know how I would have coped.

One thing I'll never fully understand is the culture of unpaid internships, especially in the nonprofit sector in the US. It's a system that excludes so many deserving people because not everyone can afford to work for free. And even for those who can, no rationale, in my opinion, ever suffi-ciently justify unpaid, skilled labor.

Just like the first internship, the four months flew by. Faster, even. Once again, despite all my efforts within and outside the organization, I couldn't secure a full-time role. Most of the rejections were tied to one thing: my visa status. I had a few interviews that never moved past the question, *"Are you authorized to work without sponsorship?"* The minute I said no, the conversation was essentially over.

I was down to my last four months when something unexpected happened.

I advanced to the next stage of a job interview, for the kind of role I had always prayed for. It was with a company I deeply admired, an organization known for its meaningful global impact, including in Nigeria. When I first saw the opening, my Impostor Syndrome sneezed to alert me of its presence. *"Would they even consider me?"* was my first thought.

But Henry, who remained by my side through every high and low, kept encouraging me to believe I had what it took to secure the job. He prepped with me, prayed with me and for me, and on the day of the interview, I nailed it. I didn't need to wait for them to call me back; I knew I had given it my best.

Soon enough, to my delight and to no one's surprise, they reached out for the next stage of the interview.

Now, this next stage was way tougher, and my confidence wavered a bit. But still, I pushed through.

Next came the invitation for the final interview. This time it was with the most senior leaders in the organization. It was exciting and scary at the same time—the kind of moment where your dream feels close enough to touch, yet fragile enough to slip away.

Something interesting also began to happen around that same period. My inbox, which had been home to silence and rejection emails, suddenly came alive. I started receiving callbacks for other interviews, and invitations for assessments. All of a sudden, I had options.

However, I was most interested in one particular opportunity: a Technical Officer II role at FHI 360. The role was a great starting point for my career, the pay was solid, and the work involved field visits to Nigeria, something I had always dreamed of. Additionally, the organization's global reputation and brand positioning could offer access to an influential network in the education and development space. I could go on and on... but the sum of it is that I was sold.

I continued attending other job assessments to keep my options open, but deep down, I knew in my heart that if FHI 360 extended an offer, I would accept it quicker than I could blink. After eight long weeks of interviews, they requested a background check. My joy knew no bounds! It was a very hopeful sign.

Oftentimes, a background check is the last step before a company makes an offer. It meant they were seriously considering me. My heart raced knowing I was closer to my dream job. This felt like what people call an *11th-hour miracle*[1].

From the second stage of the interviews, I had been upfront about my visa status because I was tired of all the past disappointments and wasted time. They told me that while no one on the team had ever been sponsored, they were open to exploring it because they believed I was a strong fit. This conversation, coupled with the background check request, gave me a lot of hope.

Two weeks later, after the background check, they finally made an offer. And it was quite generous. This came in the 10th month of my OPT visa, which, as you'll recall, was valid for one year. I had to secure a full-time role with sponsorship before it expired. So I was excited and overwhelmed with gratitude.

I heartily accepted the offer and immediately reached out to the HR team to discuss the next steps for visa sponsor-

---

1. The 11th-hour miracle is a miracle that comes at the moment when it seems like there is no more hope.

since time was running out. A few days later, the senior recruiter asked to schedule a call to discuss this. What happened after that call left me in complete shock. Here is the email I received:

Dear Odinaka,

I am very sorry about the TOII position. We are not able to sponsor a work visa for this position. I really apologize for the miscommunication. As I mentioned by phone, it might be possible for us to hire you for a position once you are back in Nigeria; however, due to our policies you would be hired and paid as a local and in local currency. If you would consider this, let us speak further about opportunities with FHI360 in Nigeria as we have proposals that we are currently working on that could potentially lead to a lot of work in Nigeria. We also have a country office there.

The feedback from the company left me in shock and utter disappointment.

I didn't know how to respond to the email. Shock, disappointment, and a sinking feeling hit me at the same time. The worst part? I had turned down every other opportunity because I was ready to commit to this organization. We had even begun discussing start dates. But just like that, everything was off the table.

As if that blow wasn't enough, the backup options I had counted on suddenly disappeared. There were no new interview callbacks, just silence. Even the rejections were not pouring in.

I was emotionally shut down, mentally drained, and physically ill. After ten long weeks in that grueling interview process, I kept asking myself, *"Why did it end like this? What could I have done differently?"*

I got advice that maybe I wasn't applying to enough jobs per day because I should at least be getting automatic rejections from companies that didn't hire international students. But there was nothing. At that moment, whatever morale or determination I had to apply for jobs simply evaporated.

Amid all the uncertainty, Nneka kept me grounded. I had started my graduate school journey in her house, and now, due to the COVID lockdown, I was ending it there too. It was a blessing to have her by my side. Her support kept me sane on the days I thought I would lose my mind from the anxiety of the whole process.

She constantly encouraged me to keep going. She would say to me, *"This too will pass. I know it seems like nothing is happening, but before you know it, this will be behind you. Take it easy, pause when you need to, and don't forget to fully live life because these days will be behind you soon."*

She cared for me in so many ways that nurtured me emotionally during that period. She was also intentional about making sure that I got out of the house once in a while to enjoy myself, even when I didn't feel like it. And oh, my little niece added so much color to the whole picture. Her laughter, constant play, and talkative nature had ways of distracting me from things that bothered me. There was also my brother-in-law, whose sense of humour never failed to make me laugh and encouraged me to keep going.

And of course, Henry.

I've already written a full chapter about him, but I must say there wasn't a single job interview he wasn't a part of. He prepped with me, prayed with me, and stayed on the line to calm my nerves. He reminded me of who I was, affirmed my worth, and his unwavering belief in me gave me the confidence I needed to face each interview.

I was surrounded by love. I just couldn't always see it through the fog of mental and emotional exhaustion. But looking back now, I realize that my support system was what held me up.

I had barely two months left, and nothing was coming forth. It was at that point that I decided I was done with NGOs.

But where do I begin?

Everything I had ever wanted to do, career-wise, was in the non-profit/NGO space. I wasn't sure how to begin navigating a different path. I was anxious, and I lacked clarity and direction. So I began trying just about everything: professional certifications, volunteering, networking events, and applying to a massive volume of jobs on LinkedIn. I even considered pivoting into tech—after all, everyone said it was the *in* thing. But all of it left me more drained than hopeful.

I reached out to friends, mentors, family members, career coaches, basically anyone I could think of, for advice. But the more advice I received, the more confused I became. Everyone had well-meaning suggestions they thought were best for my situation.

"Try Canada."

"Go back for a second master's."

"Apply for a PhD."

"Look into tech."

"Try a different visa."

Everyone meant well. But I was spinning.

I had a 60-day grace period on my OPT. During that additional time, I could stay unemployed before losing legal status. As I approached the end of this grace period, I seriously considered returning to Nigeria. I was tired and burnt out. I didn't have the mental strength to keep hoping.

But when I called home, my father, who usually encouraged me to come back after my degree, didn't sound so sure this time.

I thought to myself that things couldn't have gotten so bad in Nigeria. At least I wouldn't be battling this kind of emotional exhaustion. But with conversations back home and the End SARS crisis, I realized that the political and economic climate in Nigeria had also deteriorated in the two years I had been away. The question of *"What next?"* had never been harder to answer.

To create the illusion of progress, I offered my time volunteering with organizations, applied to countless jobs, and entertained options I had previously dismissed, like moving to Canada for a second degree. When I tried, I couldn't secure an admission. Nothing was working. I was truly exhausted.

One day, I joined a prayer meeting, and a woman said something simple that struck me. She said, *"You need to learn to trust God."* I heard that same message again at church that weekend. In fact, it became the recurring message all around me from various sources, *"You need to learn to trust God."*

So, one night, I broke down crying. *"God, how do I trust you when I can't even see?"* I was so broken and didn't realize how much I had tied my significance to achievements. *How is it that Odinaka, the Penn UNESCO and 2-time scholarship winner, couldn't even get a permanent offer after a year?* I was harder on myself than the situation warranted. But I was frustrated and confused. I went from one prayer meeting to the other, and that didn't help either. My heart just needed to be still. But I didn't know how to do that.

It was during that season that I came across Debola Deji-Kurunmi, known by many as DDK. Her teachings, rooted in scripture and strategy, helped me reconnect to purpose. Just by listening to her, my dreams started to come alive. There was never a moment of listening to DDK that didn't end with a greater sense of self-awareness and a desire to grow and mature in the things I was created for. I enrolled in the Immerse Inner Circle, one of her coaching communities, and that was a turning point in that season.

I realized that not only had COVID caused such uncertainty and anxiety within me, but that I had also gone through a high level of stress, making it difficult to see opportunities even when they appeared. Through DDK's Cleanse program in the Immerse Inner Circle, I took a break to go through a journey of soul healing. It was scary to pause, but I'm so grateful I did.

Three weeks in, I felt lighter. I could finally breathe and reflect inward instead of racing outward. I had been running so fast that I didn't realize I was out of fuel. The Cleanse program helped me build resilience, shift perspective, and slowly remember who I was becoming.

In leaning inward, I also learned to look upward. I remembered how God had carried me before I got the admission and scholarships—how He came through for me in the most unexpected ways. This was another test of trust. I also remembered the promise that anchored the start of this book: *"You saw me before I was born. Every day of my life was recorded in your book. Every moment was laid out before a single day had passed."* (Psalm 139:16 NLT).

In the ending chapters of the journey, I had to keep that verse before me.

Though everything around me was uncertain, God was

not. My job wasn't to control the timeline, but to sit with the One who had already written it. Trusting Him didn't erase the chaos, but it gave me peace, a peace I didn't know I desperately needed.

And from that peace came the clarity to begin again.

Just when I had resigned myself to returning to Nigeria without a job, I received an email:

To: You   Mon 31/01/2022 17:24

Cc: You

Hello Odinaka,

My name is Tunga Rukundo and I am a Recruiter at Catholic Relief Services. Thank you for your interest in our Leadership Development Training Coordinator II position. I would like to speak with you about your experience, and share a bit more about the position with you. Are you available for a brief phone interview on Tuesday, February 8th at 11:00am EST? Please provide an alternate time to speak if the suggested day/time does not work.

An unexpected job offer.

It was a week before my visa expired! The timing was surreal—coming at a time when I had finally come to rest in the knowledge that whatever came my way, God was on my side. It took reaching the very end of myself to truly lean in and surrender to Him.

At first, I was confused. I couldn't remember applying to the organization. But I checked my records and saw that I had submitted an application months earlier, but never heard back. It was during that season of silence when no one seemed to be getting back to me, so that made the timing feel even more miraculous.

I was excited but cautious. The organization, CRS, had long been on my radar. Their work in international development also aligned deeply with my passions, and their values mirrored mine. But I'd experienced enough disappointments to know not to cling too tightly.

To my surprise, the interview process was seamless. And within a month, I had my first full-time job (*happy tears*).

With the help of a lawyer, I was able to extend my US visa for an additional six months. And as the pieces began to fall into place, I discovered a new visa route that I was eligible for in the UK—the High Potential Individual (HPI) visa. One of the eligibility criteria was graduating from a top 50 global university, and thankfully, my degree from UPenn made me eligible. I applied, and within two weeks, it was approved.

Rather than continue pursuing a US visa sponsorship, I decided to relocate to the UK. I discussed this with my employer, and to my delight, they had no issues with me working remotely from abroad. For the first time in a long while, I felt a deep peace about my next step.

I could go on and on, narrating the *"what nexts"* of my life and what happened after those six months. But what's most important is this: Learning to trust did something profound for my soul. It gave me peace beyond understanding.

Relocating to the UK was another chapter, and a challenging one at that, but what I have learned through it all is that in every phase of life, God's grace is sufficient to bring us through. Life is in phases, and there is a certain growth, maturity, and resilience we build through each phase. The trials don't last forever, no matter how long each trying season may seem. And with each courageous step you take forward, it is an invitation to grow into strength, into surrender, and into a higher version of yourself.

*Every courageous step you take forward is an
invitation to grow into strength, into
surrender, and into a higher version
of you.*

So, if you find yourself waiting, whether it's on funding, on clarity, on *"what comes next,"* I hope you remember this: you are not forgotten, and you are not behind. Trust God with your whole heart. That's where true peace begins.

Chapter 15

We All Need Humans

Two people are better off than one, for they can help each other succeed. If one person falls, the other can reach out and help. But someone who falls alone is in real trouble (Ecclesiastes 4:9–10, NLT).

My story through graduate school and beyond is interlaced with the lives of family, friends, close acquaintances, relatives, colleagues, and classmates—people who made the journey worthwhile. Some I knew intimately, and others, like remote LinkedIn connections, I never met in person. Yet, they showed up in ways that mattered: putting in a good word, reviewing my CV, or graciously offering their time for a coffee chat.

Looking back, I'm filled with gratitude for everyone who extended kindness and generosity. Even those who didn't, in their way, taught me something about life and the people we encounter.

One truth stands out clearly: no one can do it alone. While I leaned heavily on my faith in God, I quickly learned that He works through the people He places in our lives. Graduate school was my journey, but it was far from a solitary one.

I must highlight that the pandemic added a unique layer of isolation to an already challenging period. Social distancing and virtual interactions could not fully replace the warmth of in-person connections. Yet, even in that void, I discovered that community can take many forms; from the encouraging text messages from my friends and loved ones, to the virtual study group meetings, and even brief conversations with strangers who seemed to appear at the right moment.

This chapter is a celebration of the real, and deeply human connections that sustained me. We are not made to journey through life alone—whether it's graduate school or any other season of life. We are not created to exist in isolation, but to live and thrive within a community. It is in these connections that life finds meaning.

It is also my reflection on the power of community, both the kind I craved but couldn't always access and the kind I found in unexpected places.

Finally, it's my tribute to the people who carried me in their different ways, sometimes without even knowing it. As I reach the end of this journey, allow me to share with you a few of those moments that reminded me of *just how much* we need each other.

The Friends Who Made it Feel Like Home

Elisa, a classmate who I later realized lived in the same building, was one of the first people who created a sense of warmth in my new environment. She had a geniality about her that made people feel seen and included. She'd invite me over for tea with her favorite crepe recipe, and leave thoughtful notes, cards, or chocolates for me at various times. Through those moments, she created a space that felt a little more like home. She was the one who nudged me to join the Catholic community gatherings on campus, and before I knew it, serving at Mass became something I looked forward to.

Her presence opened my world, not just to new people, but to new experiences. I still laugh when I think about her convincing me to try the vegan food spots on campus. I wasn't thrilled at first, but she insisted. To my surprise, the food was nice. Those trips, along with our coffee and doughnut dates, became little rituals that broke up the stress of school.

And in one of my lowest moments, she collaborated with my boyfriend (now husband) to send me a Valentine's Day gift. I hadn't expected it. But that simple act reminded me how deeply seen and loved I was. Elisa turned a foreign space into something that felt a little more like home.

And then, there were friends like Claudia, a classmate of mine, who opened her home to me. I remember one particular Saturday evening when she invited me over for dinner after a long week. Claudia was waiting at the door to give me a warm hug, take my coat, and get me settled into her home. That evening, I tasted shrimp ravioli for the first time, and no matter how I try, I can never quite make it the way she did.

Though it was a simple meal, I never forgot the taste of that moment. I call it a recipe made with love.

Claudia's home felt like a sanctuary, a place where I could breathe and just be. For a few hours, I would forget about assignments, deadlines, and the constant pressure of graduate school. Claudia reminded me that home isn't always a physical space—it's a feeling, and it can be created through kindness and openness.

Then, there was Aishwarya. Meeting her felt like discovering a kindred spirit. We were both international students from the Global South, navigating a new culture, a new academic environment, and the unique challenges that came with being far from home. What truly bonded us, though, was our shared background in education and grassroots development. Both of us had taught in underserved communities through the Teach For India and Teach For Nigeria fellowship programs, respectively, and those experiences gave us endless stories to exchange. We often found ourselves nodding in agreement, laughing at more than a few similarities, and even tearing up at the challenges we'd faced as international students. Through Aishwarya, I realized that shared experiences, even the difficult ones, can form the foundation of some of the most meaningful relationships.

There was also Catherine, who was a friend and a study partner for group assignments. Catherine was so warm and always willing to help. Whenever I think of Catherine, I remember her home-made brownies (*don't mind me, I am such a foodie*). I have a deep appreciation for home-made meals. It's my love language and a way into my heart. Now, every brownie I eat, wherever I am in the world, reminds me of Catherine. Months later, I reciprocated her hospitality by making my special Nigerian jollof rice for her and Aishwarya. It was a first-time experience for them, and we all enjoyed it.

The Friendships That Transcended Borders

Bola was a core friend and supporter in graduate school. It didn't matter that we were miles apart; her words had a way of making me feel less alone.

Bola and I had been friends even before graduate school, having been coursemates in our undergraduate studies in Nigeria. But there was something about this graduate school experience that brought us closer than we had ever been. She was navigating her unique experiences as an international student in Canada, and in sharing our challenges, triumphs, and occasional frustrations, we built a deep sense of understanding and camaraderie. Our friendship and communication became a 24/7 kind of thing.

Bola taught me that community isn't about proximity; it's primarily about intention. She showed me that sometimes, the right words at the right time can be as powerful as a hug or a face-to-face conversation.

The Constants in the Background

Though this chapter is about friends, I would like to talk about one of my elder sisters, the *Ada*[1] of our home, Adaeze. During grad school, she was my CEO—Chief Encouragement Officer.

During those sleepless nights spent finishing assignments, Ada was always on the other end of the call. On the

---

1. Ada is a title for the first-born daughter in the Igbo culture.

days of meal prep and culinary experiments, she was there, always ready with a recipe recommendation or a tip to make my cooking adventures smoother. When I struggled with hair *wahala*[2], trying to figure out how to manage my 4C natural hair, Ada had all the hacks.

Even though she was far away in Canada, she made the journey feel less lonely. I wish I could write about every single person I met who left an imprint on my heart during my graduate school journey. But I'd like to end this chapter with one of the soul-striking moments I had in graduate school. It was a visit from Chioma.

The Visit I Didn't Know I Needed

Chioma and I had been friends since our undergraduate days, though we hadn't always stayed in close touch. Yet, she showed up for me in a season when I felt like I was falling apart. It was those days of my favorite class—Mr. A, the professor. She flew from Colorado to Philadelphia to spend time with me. I didn't expect it to have the depth of impact it did, but that visit turned out to be everything I needed. The hugs, the laughter, the heartfelt conversations we shared, the encouragement, the prayers...everything! It felt like a true soul-sister moment.

Chioma also insisted we take some pictures around campus, and who would have thought those ordinary snapshots would become some of my last memorable moments on campus before the COVID lockdown? I had assumed there would be plenty of time to slow down and enjoy the environ-

---

2. Nigerian Pidgin expression for *"trouble"* or *"problem."*

later, but now I am grateful we captured those little moments when we did.

Chioma was the adventurous kind. I remember she once planned a road trip in Colorado, where we stayed in a rustic cabin for the night and went hiking in the mountains, only to almost get lost along the way. Those days were fun and unforgettable.

Each of these friendships, so different, yet so meaningful, helped me see that community isn't about the size of your circle; it's about the quality of the people in it. It's about those who show up in their own unique ways, making you feel seen, supported, and valued.

I'm eternally grateful for the people who remind us of who we are, who show up when life feels like too much, and who create moments that stay with us forever. My graduate school journey would not be complete without them.

Graduate school taught me many things. But perhaps the most profound lesson was this: **We all need humans.**

And I thank God for the ones who walked this part of the road with me.

Wrapping it all up

Breathe in. Out. In. Out. Now do that one more time.

If you've stayed with me to this point, I bet you can agree it's truly been a journey! And perhaps for some of you, it's even been longer, filled with the unique stories you carry, whether from graduate school or the steps you've taken toward your dream.

For me, this journey began with conviction: that there was still so much more I could be and do, that there was still room to keep learning and be challenged in new ways. Still, that conviction didn't mean I never had questions. On more than one occasion, I found myself asking, *"Who sent me?"*

Is this worth it?

Is it worth all the stress?

Is it worth the distance from home and loved ones?

Is it worth the financial sacrifice?

The decision to study abroad can often be daunting. Yet, it's a decision that can change everything.

When I think back to the days of applications and the joy of finally getting into graduate school with scholarships, I can't help but laugh. I laugh when I remember how much I stressed over things that eventually worked out. And I laugh because I had absolutely no clue how much this experience—short as I thought it would be—was going to change me.

What's most important is that I now see clearly how God showed up in ways I could never have scripted. And how every challenge I overcame became a reminder of the resilience within me.

Sometimes, we romanticise the idea of growth. We imagine it happens when we stay in our comfort zones, but the real growth happens when we step out—when we dare to try new things, risk failing, and enter spaces that stretch us. And the graduate journey will 100% do that; it will widen your capacity in ways you might scarcely have anticipated.

If I had to do it again, I'd gladly embrace the opportunity because it brought about a version of myself I'm proud of today:

- The resilient woman who learned to trust God amid setbacks and uncertainties.
- The woman who finally understood that her worth was never tied to her achievements.

- The woman who became confident, knowing there are no limits to what her mind can learn or achieve.

That's why I'm reminded that the graduate journey is never just about degrees or careers. It has a way of reshaping us, of bringing about an evolution of self—and that is a good thing.

Today, I work in a role that brings together my passion for education, international development, and leadership. I now support brilliant African scholars, many of whom are navigating journeys that mirror mine, and I consider it a privilege to be a part of their story.

Wherever you are on your own journey, may this book remind you that your story is still unfolding.

So, breathe again. In. Out.

Now trust the process. Trust God. And keep walking.

Graduate Journey Toolkit

This Toolkit contains practical guidance to help you on your graduate journey. You will find guides, templates, trackers, and other resources to make your journey easy.

Simply scan the QR code below and dive in.

Or go to: **Odinakachukwu.com/toolkit**

Author Note

Dear Reader,

I don't take it lightly that you've spent time here with me. When I first began writing, I didn't know this would become a book with two parts! Honestly, I just needed a space to process the experiences that had stretched and reshaped so much of my life in such a short time.

Back then, it started as short, scrappy notes—more like a journal or raw material for a podcast—nothing like what you're holding in your hands right now. But a few years down the line, after graduation, I felt a nudge to return to it and continue writing. And as I began again, I understood why.

This book was meant to bless others, especially those navigating their own transition into graduate life. I've never poured my heart into a project as I have with this one, and that's because of *you*. I wanted to give you something that could become your own keepsake memoir. I truly hope I've done that.

If you'd like to stay connected, I share conversations

beyond this book on my social media pages and newsletter. You can find links to them on my website, <u>odinakachukwu.com.</u> (You'll also find my podcast linked there). You'll be sure to find the same heart there: a life focused on faith, purpose, and intentional living.

I'd love to hear from you, too. What did this book stir in you? How has your own journey been?

Before I go, let me leave you with this blessing:

May your journey remind you that the waiting is not wasted.

May your faith grow stronger in the places that feel uncertain.

May your friendships become anchors in seasons of loneliness.

May your vision stretch wider than the classroom or the degree.

And may you never forget that the One who called you is faithful to complete the work He began in you.

Thank you for reading. I mean that with all my heart.

About the Book

The Graduate Journey: Lessons, Growth & Grace is a reflective guide for young people leaving home in pursuit of an excellent education and new opportunities abroad. International students navigating life in a new world will see their experiences mirrored here, while aspiring students will find a map for their own paths.

Through Odinaka's story, being the first Nigerian to win the fully-funded Penn-UNESCO scholarship, studying at an Ivy League institution, and carving out a place for herself far from home, this book pulls back the curtain on what it takes to build resilience, what graduate life truly looks like, and how to emerge with clarity, strategy, and purpose.

Raw, relatable, and refreshingly honest, this book reveals the challenges no one warns you about while shining a light on the possibilities that lie ahead.

Inside, you'll find:

- Unfiltered stories of studying abroad, told from lived experience.

- Encouragement for the *"What's next?"* seasons of doubt and transition.
- Practical tips on scholarships, job searches, relationships, and well-being.
- A free downloadable Toolkit packed with resources (from scholarship application templates to a settling down manual) to guide your own journey.

About the Author

Odinaka Chukwu Anumudu is a leadership development professional with a heart for education and a vision to see young Africans lead with purpose.

She has experience across education, international development, global scholarship programs, and leadership development, and currently supports high-achieving African scholars in navigating academic and career transitions.

Odinaka holds a Master's degree in International Educational Development from the University of Pennsylvania, where she studied as a Penn-UNESCO Fellow and P.E.O. International Peace Scholar.

Writing and mentoring from a place of lived experiences, she helps others navigate transitions with empathy, clarity, and faith.

The Graduate Journey is her debut book—a reflective, personal yet practical guide for dreamers, doers, and those learning to trust God in the waiting.

Connect with her on Instagram @odinaka_ and LinkedIn at linkedin.com/in/odinaka-chukwu